Redacted Dominionism

Redacted Dominionism

A Biblical Approach to Grounding Environmental Responsibility

CHRISTOPHER CONE

WIPF & STOCK · Eugene, Oregon

REDACTED DOMINIONISM
A Biblical Approach to Grounding Environmental Responsibility

Wipf & Stock
An Imprint of Wipf and Stock Publishers
199 W. 8th Ave., Suite 3
Eugene, OR 97401

www.wipfandstock.com

ISBN 13: 978-1-62032-159-1

This book is dedicated to my beloved Cathy, Christiana, and Cara Grace—three lovely ladies whose remarkable patience and sacrifice made this work possible; to my brothers and sisters whose prayers carried this project through; and most of all, to my precious Lord, whose creation I am, and whose glory I seek.

This is my Father's world . . .

Contents

Acknowledgments

SPECIAL THANKS TO DRS. Patrick and Armida Belvill for your constant encouragement and faithful prayer especially during this project; to Dr. Charles Ryrie, for your example, encouragement, and friendship; and to each and every member of the staff and faculty at Tyndale Theological Seminary—your diligence and dedication is a daily inspiration and encouragement to me.

Sincerest gratitude to Dr. J. Baird Callicott, Dr. Sarah E. Fredericks, and Dr. Martin Yaffe of the University of North Texas Philosophy & Religion Studies Department, for your patience and determination in seeing this project through. I am indebted to each of you, and very grateful for the time you invested in me.

Abbreviations

BDB Francis Brown, Samuel Rolles Driver, and Charles Augustus Briggs. *Enhanced Brown-Driver-Briggs Hebrew and English Lexicon, electronic ed.* Oak Harbor, WA: Logos Research Systems, 2000.

BHS *Biblia Hebraica Stuttgartensia: With Westminster Hebrew Morphology*. Electronic ed. Stuttgart; Glenside PA: German Bible Society; Westminster Seminary, 1996, c1925; morphology c1991.

EC Evangelical community

ESV English Standard Version Bible. Wheaton, IL: Crossway Books, 2001.

HB Hebrew Bible

LXX Septuaginta: With Morphology. Stuttgart: Deutsche Bibelgesellschaft, 1996, c1979.

NA27 Barbara Aland, Kurt Aland, Matthew Black et al. *The Greek New Testament*. 4th ed. Federal Republic of Germany: United Bible Societies, 1993, c1979.

NASB New American Standard Bible. 1995 Update. LaHabra, CA: Lockman Foundation, 1995.

NT New Testament

1

Tension Between Evangelical and Environmental Thought

In a September 2008 article titled, "Evangelicals Go 'Green' with Caution," The Barna Group discusses the results of a study pertaining to evangelical attitudes toward the environment.[1] For purposes of the study, The Barna Group, which is itself positioned within the evangelical community, characterizes evangelicals as those who "met the born again criteria . . . plus seven other conditions . . . saying their religious faith is very important in their life today; believing they have a personal responsibility to share their religious beliefs about Christ with non-Christians; believing that Satan exists; believing that eternal salvation is possible only through grace, not works; believing that Jesus Christ lived a sinless life on earth; asserting that the Bible is accurate in all that it teaches; and describing God as the all-knowing, all-powerful, perfect deity who created the universe and still rules it today."[2] For the sake of simplicity and clarity, despite its obvious limitations, this characterization will be assumed in all following references to the term "evangelical."[3]

1. According to their website, "Barna Group is a visionary research and resource company . . . widely considered to be the leading research organization focused on the intersection of faith and culture." Barna Group, "About Barna Group."

2. Barna Group, "Evangelicals Go 'Green.'"

3. For the sake of disclosure, though not preferring the term—with its stereotypes and negative connotations—this writer agrees, at least in principle, with each of these ideas, and may thus be described as a member of the evangelical community. The

The Barna Group's study finds that "millions of [American] evangelicals—often perceived to be on the sidelines of the green movement—have recently become more environmentally conscious. Yet evangelicals do so with some skepticism about the environmental movement."[4] The study notes skepticism on the part of evangelicals in three particular areas: (1) concern about media hype regarding global warming; (2) doubts about the role of humans in climate change; and (3) concern that proposed solutions would harm people, especially the poor in developing nations.[5] The study finds that 90 percent of evangelicals "would like Christians to take a more active role in caring for creation," though only 27 percent firmly believe that global warming is happening.[6] These two statistics, considered together are telling, as they reflect a willingness on the part of evangelicals to consider the importance of environmental issues, while at the same time underscoring a suspicious posture on the part of evangelicals toward at least aspects of the environmental movement.

It might be taken for granted that, because the evangelical community (EC) already shares a fairly high level of concern, the remedial focus—if the perceived immobility of the EC is to be overcome in favor of a more environmentally friendly perspective—should be to raise awareness within that community regarding the seriousness of ecological crises. Still, this writer suggests that those outside the EC should consider another approach altogether.

Earlier critiques of Christian attitudes toward the environment were leveled not at the amount of data adherents of the Christian worldview possessed, but rather at core interpretive mechanisms of the worldview itself. Popular literature has driven a wedge between environmental concerns and Christianity, not necessarily by suggesting that Christians lack understanding of the ecological consequences of dumping toxic waste in rivers, for example, but by suggesting that Christians believe they have theological warrant for environmental irresponsibility. The popular narrative has been that the Bible does not provide a suitable grounding for environmental responsibility, and that its adherents must

writer's hope is that this project will inform and invigorate those within the evangelical community to greater responsibility, and encourage those outside the evangelical community to engage in dialogue more understanding of evangelical methodology and perspectives, for a more productive discussion.

4. Barna, "Evangelicals Go 'Green.'"

5. Ibid.

6. Ibid.

seek an alternative grounding if they are to be ecologically considerate. It should come as no surprise that the environmental gospel has been met by the EC with skepticism. The popular critiques to this point have largely demanded a worldview reconstruction that is simply incompatible with a community that believes that "the Bible is accurate in all that it teaches."[7] Notable among many others, Aldo Leopold, Ian McHarg, and Lynn White all question, to differing extents, the Bible's contribution to environmental concerns.

Aldo Leopold was a forester and game manager, by profession, whose book, *A Sand County Almanac*, became "the bible" of the emerging environmental movement and the seminal text for the advent of environmental ethics in academic philosophy. Leopold laments that "our Abrahamic concept of land" was wholly incompatible with conservation ideas.[8] He elaborates in a later context that, according to the biblical concept of land, "Land . . . is still property."[9] He views the Decalogue as beneficial in relating individual to individual, and the Golden Rule as relating the individual to society, but asserts that, even though Ezekiel and Isaiah spoke negatively regarding despoliation of land, there has not yet been affirmed (in the Bible or anywhere else) an ethic relating man to land, animal, and plant.[10] It seems no overstatement to say that he perceives the Christian worldview to be systemically deficient in the realm of environmental concerns. In Leopold's estimation, it seems the Bible contributes to an environmental apathy and provides no ethic to remedy the ailment. Further, Leopold's pronouncement that "only the most superficial student of history supposes that Moses 'wrote' the Decalogue; it evolved in the minds of a thinking community, and Moses wrote a tentative summary of it for a 'seminar'"[11] illustrates that his vantage point is from a worldview that does not consider the Bible as the product of divine inspiration—a position incompatible with that of the EC.

Ian McHarg's comments are not unlike Leopold's, though they are certainly more pointed and strident. As an influential landscape architect and writer, involved in both theoretical and practical aspects of environmental planning, he critiques the "Western

7. Ibid.

8. Leopold, *Sand County Almanac*, viii.

9. Ibid., 203.

10. Ibid., 202–3.

11. Ibid., 225.

anthropocentric-anthropomorphic tradition in which nature is relegated to inconsequence."[12] He acknowledges, like Leopold, that Judaism and Christianity have shown concern for the relationships of man to man, but have been of little or no benefit in dealing with man and nature relationships, especially because, McHarg alleges, the Judeo-Christian worldview has "traditionally assumed nature to be a mere backdrop for the human play."[13] He credits the literally interpreted Genesis creation account as representing "man [as] exclusively divine, man given dominion over all life and nonlife, enjoined to subdue the earth."[14] The world has merely instrumental value in supporting man's drama, and "reality exists only because man can perceive it."[15]

Lynn White Jr. was a historian of medieval technology. His famed and controversial 1967 paper, "The Historical Roots of our Ecologic Crisis" perhaps best illustrates that early critiques were incompatible with foundational tenets of the EC, as it launched a scathing critique of certain religious underpinnings of Western attitude toward nature, and was met with immediate enthusiasm by those already suspicious (to say the least) of doctrinal tenets that seemed to ground Western thought firmly in anthropocentrism.[16] White's essay "implicitly set the theoretical agenda for a future environmental philosophy,"[17] in a number of ways, and remains profoundly influential if only as a provocative point of entry for discussion of environmental ethics.[18] Creditable initially to White's evaluation of the Judeo-Christian ethic and of Christianity, the perception that Christianity is culpable for environmental destruction and has proven useless in countering that destruction has become a cliché in the environmental movement.[19]

Though White indicts Christianity as a primary culprit for environmental degradation, it is not readily apparent whether he is critiquing

12. McHarg, "Place of Nature," 1–12.

13. Ibid., 4.

14. Ibid.

15. Ibid.

16. The paper was first read in December 1966 at a meeting of the American Association for the Advancement of Science, and was subsequently published several months later in the journal *Science* as Lynn Townsend White Jr., "The Historical Roots of Our Ecologic Crisis," 1203–7.

17. Callicott, "Genesis Revisited," 65.

18. Fox, *American Conservation Movement*, 359.

19. Berry, "Survival of Creation," 53.

only particular aspects of Christian experience, community, tradition, or textual grounding as individual components, or whether he is appraising all of these collectively. Peter Harrison describes White's project as focusing on "what the text was taken to mean at certain periods of history, how it motivated specific activities, and how it came to sanction a particular attitude toward the natural world."[20]

The evidence of White's essay confirms that Harrison's understanding is well founded. White introduces his discussion with the admission of limited knowledge of the true cause of or severity of the ecological crisis, saying, "The history of ecological change is still so rudimentary that we know little about what really happened, or what the results were."[21] In light of the uncertainty, there is at first no suggestion for coping with the problem. Asking and answering his own important question, he remarks, "What shall we do? No one yet knows" (ibid., 1204). White blames "the presuppositions that underlie modern technology and science," and suggests the current crisis is "the product of an emerging, entirely novel, democratic culture." He questions "whether a democratized world can survive its own implications," and concludes that "presumably we cannot unless we rethink our axioms" (ibid.).

By axioms, it seems that White means first principles or presuppositions. If so, then what presuppositions does White indict? As a medieval historian he traces the roots of science and technology to the Middle Ages, suggesting accordingly that "it would seem that we cannot understand their nature or their present impact upon ecology without examining medieval assumptions and developments" (1205). Those assumptions and developments, he suggests, are rooted in "ruthlessness toward nature," and he traces this ruthlessness to the view that "man and nature are two things, and man is master" (ibid.).

Further, White traces the Western understanding of the man/nature dichotomy and hierarchy to religion. He asserts, "Human ecology is deeply conditioned by beliefs about our nature and destiny—that is religion," though he does not critique religion in general (ibid.). Rather, White points an accusing finger at one tradition directly: "The victory of Christianity over paganism was the greatest psychic revolution in the history of our culture" (1207). His indictment intensifies as he warns, "We shall continue to have a worsening ecologic crisis until we reject

20. Harrison, "Subduing the Earth," 89.

21. White, "Historical Roots," 1203.

the Christian axiom that nature has no reason for existence save to serve man" (ibid.). In assuming that Western Christianity holds to the axiom as a core belief, White offers a choice: reject the Genesis worldview (as described by White) in favor of a view like that of Francis of Assisi, or continue to act in a way that is environmentally destructive. Because White's proposed solution is less than Bible-based, it is not one that should expect to be lauded by the EC. However, there are other options besides those White offers. I propose that there is a Christian environmental ethic consistent with the core beliefs of the EC: namely, redacted dominionism, which I define in the next section.

White's is not a condemnation of Judeo-Christian tradition in its entirety, but is instead a firm denunciation of an axiom he readily identifies with the ethical traditions of Christianity (and the pedagogy and behavior that results from the alleged axiom). He denounces the Christian *worldview* as singularly culpable, and acknowledges that worldview to be "shaped by the Judeo-Christian dogma of creation" (1206). White's critical eye is turned toward Genesis, the textual grounding of the Judeo-Christian dogma of creation. He suggests that Christianity inherited from Judaism "a striking story of creation," and he makes claims about what the creation story says and claims about how the creation story has motivated and directed its adherents (1205). In particular, he makes seven relevant claims regarding implications of Genesis (1203–7). The sum of White's claims is that Christianity is inherently anthropocentric. Since he believes that anthropocentrism is not compatible with an environmental ethic, he concludes that we will not resolve the present ecological crisis "until we find a new religion, or rethink our old one" (1206).

White's recommendations that those in the Christian community recognize deficiencies in the Genesis perspective on environmental responsibility, and that the community must seek alternate means of grounding environmental ethics ought not be expected to be well received in the EC, among people who consider the Bible to be authoritative in all matters of Christian life (cf. John 17:17 and 2 Tim 3:16–17). One would expect White's to be an unacceptable exhortation. Despite his own Judeo-Christian perspective, his recommendations are premised on interpretations of Genesis that do not generally resonate within the EC. Though the EC is at times guilty of ascribing to the idea that nature exists to serve human interests, the Genesis account may be understood, within EC methodology, to show that the axiom White identifies is not textually (biblically) necessary, and consequently, a biblical environmental ethic may be derived that denies the axiom altogether.

Laurel Kearns rightly suggests that, of three prominent "Christian-related eco-theological ethics," the EC seeks to ground itself more on correct doctrine (in contrast to other groups which more emphasize praxis and spirituality), using the Bible as the primary authority, while other groups within the Christian community rely more heavily on other sources of authority, such as theological matrixes (e.g., liberation theology), social sciences and even medieval metaphysics.[22] Millard Erickson illustrates the EC emphasis of biblical authority when he observes, "When we discuss concern about the world and the entire environment, we must first try to ascertain what God says about it . . . must ascertain the true teachings of Scripture on these matters."[23]

The EC is unique among other Christian communities in that it claims reliance on the biblical text above any other spiritual or theological authority, perceiving the Bible to be God's exclusive descriptive and prescriptive revelation for this age. It might be fair to say, then, that if it is to maintain its highest order principles, the EC *must* reject mandates like White's. While White does encourage Judeo-Christian adherents to rethink their axioms, the model he provides is incompatible with the EC on two levels: (1) it assumes the premise that the Genesis account is not to be understood as literal history, and (2) it elevates praxis over doctrine—working from a proposed solution backward to its justification, rather than beginning with the biblical data and letting the chips fall where they may. Additionally, White's critiques are not entirely consistent with an EC reading of Genesis. Furthermore, his own proposed Christian solution (follow Francis of Assisi as a model of godliness, at least in environmental concerns) is deficient for reaching the EC because Francis does not provide a biblical grounding for responsibility. If the EC is to be spurred to action, it will only be if that action is understood to be biblically justified, indeed biblically mandated. While White's proposal might resonate in other religious communities, his language is particularly foreign to the EC worldview. If this is so, then critiques along the lines of White's, despite his lauding of Francis of Assisi, might not be as productive as intended—at least not for the purpose of invigorating the

22. See Kearns, "Saving the Creation," 56. Kearns cites the Christian stewardship ethic, the eco-justice ethic, and the creation spirituality ethic.

23. Erickson, "Biblical Theology of Ecology," 36–37.

EC, in particular, to heightened ecological consideration. A different approach could be helpful to that end.

Environmental philosopher J. Baird Callicott seems to recognize, as does White, that more than critiques are needed if religious communities are to share "a common ecological conscience drawn from the international scientific worldview."[24] His approach considers and encourages environmentally sympathetic themes within religious traditions around the globe. He does not ask that adherents of those traditions abandon or reject the bases of their worldviews, but rather that they emphasize the ecologically supportive elements of those worldviews. He affirms that, "we shall need some common environmental attitudes and values on which to base a common vision of a whole and healthy world."[25] Whether or not Callicott's idea of a common vision is an achievable goal—or even a tolerable one to the various traditions he discusses—is not the germane point here. What is relevant to the matter at hand is that Callicott's approach illustrates a mood shift in the discussion, from the outright condemnations in the early popular literature (e.g., Leopold and McHarg) to the worldview challenges White poses to the EC, to a more irenic and inclusive dialogue. Make no mistake; Callicott's purpose is to spread the gospel of environmental responsibility where that gospel has previously not penetrated. Still, even if certain aspects of Callicott's thesis and various premises may not be entirely agreeable to the EC, there is a clear advantage in his efforts to understand the various religious traditions he discusses, and in his desire to tease out of each tradition an environmental ethic. For those seeking to harness the energy of the EC for the environmental cause, and who may or may not be otherwise unsympathetic to EC ideas, the present project promises to provide tools to that end. To emphasize the point sufficiently, it is worth repeating here: in general the EC responds to biblical mandates, and if the EC understands environmental responsibility as a biblical mandate, the EC will respond.

The project at hand is premised on the idea that within the EC specifically, exhortations to discard or deemphasize the Bible as God's exclusive descriptive and prescriptive revelation for this age in order to generate environmental responsibility will not be as effective to that end as would simple heightened attentiveness be in applying principles already commonly assented to within the EC. These principles include the

24. Callicott, *Earth's Insights*, xvi.

25. Ibid.

idea that the Bible is authoritative in its descriptions and prescriptions, and the idea that they should be interpreted literally—or more specifically, with a literal grammatical-historical hermeneutic. Though there is disagreement within the EC regarding the hermeneutics of biblical predictive prophecy, the literal grammatical-historical hermeneutic has been considered within the EC as the best hermeneutic for understanding the Bible: with *literal* referencing a propositional, plain-sense approach; *grammatical* emphasizing that the rules of the language employed are to be observed and followed in the interpretation; and *historical* connoting that the plain-sense and grammatical aspects are to be understood as they were typically understood in the historical context in which the text in question was penned. More beneficial for the environmental discussion than arguing against the EC's recognition of biblical authority and hermeneutic methodology might be a consideration of what fruit these principles actually bear in application to environmental concerns. In this case it may be better to work within the framework of the worldview than to ask its adherents to abandon it altogether, as White's proposal requires.

Beyond investigating what the Bible, read from within the EC context, indicates about the environment, this project will also seek to answer the central questions raised by Leopold, McHarg, and White in their critiques of the Genesis-based worldview. Namely, whether or not man has dominion over nature and whether or not the world was designed with anthropocentrism as a defining principle, and consequently whether or not such a worldview is antithetical to environmental concerns. The focus of this project is to respond to these questions with answers that are most consistent with the presuppositions and methodology of the EC, to the ends that the EC can be both reinforced in its core beliefs and invigorated toward environmental consideration, and that those outside the EC can have a more effective approach than has been exhibited in the past for interacting with the EC regarding environmental concerns.

2

Evangelical Presuppositions and Methodology

Evangelicalism has been described as a sub tradition of Christianity, and sub traditions are characterized as those groups that latch "on to a particular emphasis, configuration, priority, or central theme of Christianity."[1] The term *evangelical* is derived from the Greek *euangellion*, a word that means good news, and is often translated in English Bibles as *gospel*. The label emphasizes the gospel as the central emphasis of this particular sub tradition of Christianity, and has historically been applied to Christians as early as the mid-eighteenth century.[2]

Whereas in Europe the term has come to be synonymous with *Protestant*,[3] in America the term has come to be associated with specific emphases within Protestantism, as evangelicals emphasize the connection to God through the Bible more than other Protestant groups that maintain at least some commitment to "mediation of sacramental grace, tradition, and ecclesiastical authority."[4] At least from shortly after the Revolutionary War up to the Civil War, America's "ethos was predominantly evangelical."[5] By the early 1900s, the contrast between evangelicalism and

1. Mead and Hill, *Handbook of Denominations*, 251.
2. Ibid., 254.
3. Enns, *Moody Handbook of Theology*, 611.
4. Mead and Hill, *Handbook of Denominations*, 254.
5. Noll, *History of Christianity*, 222.

other Protestant groups was becoming more apparent, as evangelicals came to recognize that "God was much more accessible and his truth more readily defined than was taught by the Methodists and Presbyterians."[6] Evangelicals are recognized as more literal and propositional than other groups in their interpretation of the Bible. The presupposition that God is accessible through the Bible, and that it contains propositional revelation would obviously bear methodological fruit, as evangelicals have come to be known as "Christians who oppose some things because they affirm other things."[7]

Perhaps the most foundational affirmation of the EC is illustrated in the doctrinal statement of the Evangelical Theological Society: "The Bible alone, and the Bible in its entirety, is the Word of God written and is therefore inerrant in the autographs."[8] Evangelical philosopher Norman Geisler acknowledges that this doctrine is presuppositional and that it has consequences in methodology, also recognizing that philosophical approaches within evangelicalism vary to some extent, but warns that evangelicals must be sure that "our philosophical approach is not inconsistent with Biblical revelation or with what is presupposed by it."[9] If biblical inerrancy and authority is so foundational to the EC, it is no wonder that critiques like those of Leopold, McHarg, and White do not resonate positively within the EC, and that EC presuppositions are so distasteful to the likes of Leopold and McHarg.

If the Bible is perceived by the EC as propositional revelation, then the resulting hermeneutic methodology is no surprise. One text on evangelical hermeneutics, in discussing "that system of hermeneutics which most generally characterizes conservative Protestantism," affirms, "the divine inspiration of the Bible is the foundation of historic Protestant hermeneutics and exegesis."[10] It explains that the biblical interpreter shares with the classicist "the problem of determining the text, of translating, and of stating ancient concepts in their modern counterparts," and adds that an additional spiritual dimension must be considered, in light of the doctrine of inspiration.[11] As a result of that spiritual aspect, the

6. Mead and Hill, *Handbook of Denominations*, 254–55.

7. Ibid., 255.

8. Evangelical Theological Society, "Doctrinal Basis."

9. Geisler, *Inerrancy*, 334.

10. Ramm, *Protestant Biblical Interpretation*, ix, 93.

11. Ibid.

evangelical interpreter "severs company with . . . rationalism," in favor of "a full-fledged, intelligent Biblicism . . . adequate to the present day situation in science, philosophy, psychology, and religion."[12] Bernard Ramm is not suggesting here that the EC is irrational or antirational—on the contrary, the EC is concerned with issues of consistency, coherence, and cogency; rather he is asserting that rationalism (in the Cartesian sense) does not properly account for the limitations of human reason (such as the noetic effects of sin at the Fall), and that divine revelation provides reliable guidance in instances where the fallen mind falters.[13] He reckons that it follows that the various disciplines are best considered in the light of biblical revelation.

Further, Ramm observes that the EC does not ignore matters of higher and lower criticism and problems of translation, recognizing that "the boundary of Scripture must be determined," and that by textual criticism the efforts are "to determine what was the original wording."[14] Rather the EC approaches the disciplines of textual criticism and translation assuming, based on internal textual claims, that the text to be analyzed is divinely inspired.[15] Of course this begs the question: does the EC belief in divine revelation flirt with circular reasoning? If the claim being made is that the Bible is the word of God because it claims to be the word of God, and that claims in the text are true because the text is the word God, then this is no more than special pleading or circular reasoning. However, the EC methodology for determining the authority and boundaries of the text is a bit more nuanced than that. Geisler and Nix, and F. F. Bruce for example, suggest that the canon recognized by the EC is understood not from ecumenical councils, but from Jesus's stamp of approval,[16] which they find in (virtually[17]) every book in the current Protestant canon,

12. Ibid., 94, 95.

13. Noetic effects are those having to do with the mind and thought.

14. Ramm, *Protestant Biblical Interpretation*, 8, 9.

15. Ibid., 7.

16. Geisler and Nix, *General Introduction to the Bible*, 204ff; and F. F. Bruce, *Canon of Scripture*, 18ff. Evidenced by Jesus's identification of the text in question as authoritative (e.g., Luke 24:44–45; John 5:39, 45–46), his direct commissioning of biblical writers (e.g., John 16:12–13; Acts 1:8; Acts 9), and in a few instances, those he commissioned approving other writers (e.g., 2 Tim 4:11; 2 Pet 3:2, 15). This EC view of canonicity is explored in detail in Wenham, "Christ's View of Scripture," 6ff.

17. There is a possible exception. The Epistle to the Hebrews does not name its writer, and its inclusion in the canon was debated in the early church, but it has made its way into the canon primarily on the basis of early positive response, agreement with

and which they do not find in the apocryphal books, for example, or the Gnostic gospels, to name a few. This works, of course, because the EC considers Jesus to be divine, part of the Trinity.

To illustrate the EC understanding of Jesus's approval of the canon, several points are worth noting here. The record of Jesus's comments in Luke 11:50–51 are understood by the EC as an acknowledgement of the threefold division (Torah, Nevi'im, Ketuvim) of the Hebrew Bible—specifically in referencing Genesis as the first book and Chronicles as the last (by referencing the blood of Abel and the blood of Zechariah). The Masoretic text of the Hebrew Bible (as early as the ninth century AD/CE), maintaining the threefold division, reflects this order of books, and finds agreement with Dead Sea Scrolls from the second century BC/BCE. Further, as to Jesus's authority in the New Testament, the EC relies primarily on commissions such as those found in John 16 and Acts 1 and 9.

The EC, in its churches and seminaries, has to date given attention to working with original language (Hebrew, Aramaic, and Greek) manuscripts, and consequently EC scholarship has perhaps focused less on translation than on other aspects of textual criticism and interpretation. Still EC scholars are responsible in part for respected translations including the New American Standard Bible (NASB), and the English Standard Version (ESV). The ESV, for example, claims to be an "'essentially literal' translation that seeks as far as possible to capture the precise wording of the original text and the personal style of each Bible writer," and adds that "each word and phrase in the ESV has been carefully weighed against the original Hebrew, Aramaic, and Greek, to ensure the fullest accuracy and clarity and to avoid under-translating or overlooking any nuance of the original text."[18] The foreword to the NASB identifies the twofold purpose of the translation: "to adhere as closely as possible to the original languages of the Holy Scriptures, and to make the translation in a fluent and readable style according to current English usage."[19]

The NASB and ESV rely in large part on Kittel's *Biblia Hebraica Stuttgartensia* (BHS) and the Nestle-Aland *Greek New Testament* (GNT), both of which are in the critical text tradition—which examines all extant manuscripts and scrutinizes them in light of internal and external evidence. Though the critical text method is not universally accepted in

other biblical writings, and traditional views of authorship.

18. Schwandt and Collins, *English-Greek Reverse Interlinear New Testament*, vii.

19. Ryrie, *Ryrie Study Bible*, viii.

the EC (there remains a strong contingent committed to the King James Version, which relies on a far less critical method of translation), it is the primary approach of EC scholarship. As such, the BHS and GNT are utilized extensively in this project as need for consulting the original languages arises.

As issues of textual criticism, translation, and interpretation are considered, Ramm prescribes "the utmost care and scruples to discover the true text of both Testaments, to discover the true rules of interpretation, and to apply them with the greatest of pains and care that the word of man may not be intruded into the Word of God."[20] In short, the EC expects, begin by discerning the true text of the Bible, insofar as extant manuscript copies are reflective of the originals, and then by the application of certain principles, to arrive at an interpretation that understands the author's intent.

The writer adds that these processes do "not indulge in the wholesale reconstruction of texts, histories, and documents which characterizes liberalism."[21] (Leopold's, McHarg's and White's critiques strike a nerve here.) It should be noted at this point that whether or not those outside the EC believe there is a *true text* to be arrived at, or that it can be arrived at through textual criticism and then understood by literal translation and a literal hermeneutic, is not relevant to the matter at hand—the issue is that the EC, almost by definition, assents to these key ideas. To exhort those within the EC to abandon these foundational tenets seems an ineffective way to motivate them to action.

The EC perceives that a literal hermeneutic approach is a critical piece in understanding *the true text*. Ramm offers three defenses of the literal method: that it is "the usual practice in the interpretation of literature," that "all secondary meanings of documents depend upon the literal stratum of language," and that "only in the priority of literal exegesis is there control on the exegetical abuse of Scripture."[22] Another evangelical hermeneutic text describes, with greater specificity, that "a normal reading of Scripture is synonymous with a consistent literal, grammatico-historical hermeneutic."[23] By this is meant that the literal, grammatico (or grammatical) historical approach should be considered the normative

20. Ramm, *Protestant Biblical Interpretation*, 93.

21. Ibid.

22. Ibid., 123, 124.

23. Couch, *Classical Evangelical Hermeneutics*, 33.

approach for interpreting the Bible. The text explains that when this hermeneutic is applied, "every word of Scripture is given the normal meaning it would have in its normal usage."[24] At points, determining the *normal* usage presents challenges, even to the simplistic approach of the EC, but it should be noted that these writers use the word *normal* in reference to interpretation to indicate *normative* or even *proper*. They are suggesting that there is a right way (normal) and a wrong way to approach the text, and that if the correct methodology is not employed, the true (or intended) meaning will not be discovered by the interlocutor.

Consider for example John 1:1, which reads: "In the beginning was the word and the word was with God, and the word was God." The term translated as *word* is the Greek λόγος, which has various usages in Classical, Attic, and Koine Greek. In Koine, the noun has been understood to have a number of meanings, including *a word, a question, a preaching, a prophecy, a command, an assertion or declaration, a conversation, reason, motive*, etc.[25] There are also numerous concepts associated with and implications of the Classical and Attic usages of the term.

Ascertaining the normal usage requires a larger sample size of John's writing, and perhaps a consideration of broader contexts if more immediate contexts do not resolve the issue. John 1:14 says that the λόγος became flesh. John 2:22 says that the disciples believed τῷ λόγῳ (dative/locative noun with article) that Jesus had spoken to them. John 4:37 says the λόγος is true, that "one sows and another reaps." The normal usage in the early part of John's gospel is *saying* or *word*, but clearly something beyond that is being addressed in John 1:1 and 1:14. An earlier NT writer says, "God, after He spoke long ago to the fathers in the prophets in many portions and in many ways, in these last days has spoken to us in His Son. . . . " (Heb 1:1–2).[26] The author of Hebrews perceived Jesus as the revelation of God personified. If so, then John's reference to Jesus as λόγος might best be translated *word*, and might further indicate that John also perceived Jesus to be God's revelation personified. That could also explain how the λόγος was said to have become flesh (John 1:14).

This is an example of how the EC might apply textual criticism to a passage to resolve a translation difficulty, and it illustrates further a principle commonly applied within the framework of the literal

24. Ibid.

25. Arndt and Gingrich, *Greek-English Lexicon*, 478–80.

26. Hebrews was presumed by EC scholars to have been written about twenty years prior to John.

grammatical-historical hermeneutic—the analogy of faith.[27] The phrase was inferred from Romans 12:6, and employed by Augustine to resolve ambiguities in the text. His view is that "the general rule being, that whatever can be shown to be in its literal sense inconsistent either with purity of life or correctness of doctrine must be taken figuratively."[28] He elaborates, suggesting that as one investigates obscure passages, the interlocutor should "draw examples from the plainer expressions to throw light upon the more obscure, and use the evidence of passages about which there is no doubt to remove all hesitation in regard to the doubtful passages."[29] Further, he prescribes, "if when attention is given to the passage, it shall appear to be uncertain . . . let the reader consult the rule of faith which he has gathered from the plainer passages of Scripture"[30] While Augustine originally intended the analogy of faith as a means of distinguishing between literal and figurative intended meanings, the Reformers, and later the EC has adjusted it slightly to mean that scripture interprets scripture—that broader contexts can contribute to the interpretation of an immediate context. Paul Lee Tan describes the analogy of faith as "based on the observation that there is no better interpreter of Scripture than the Scripture itself."[31] Tan further suggests, "The analogy of faith is a foundational principle and a basic presupposition in Scriptural interpretation."[32]

While the same basic presuppositions and methodology are employed by the EC as a whole, there is variation within the EC regarding the scope of application of the literal grammatical-historical hermeneutic method. At least three major traditions are presently discernible within the EC—dispensationalism, covenant (or reformed) theology, and progressive dispensationalism—and they are distinguished primarily by the degree to which they apply the hermeneutic method.

Robert Lightner defines dispensationalism as, "that system of theology which sees the Bible as the unfolding of the distinguishable

27. Higher criticism in this case considers that the Epistle to the Hebrews predated John's gospel by twenty or more years, while lower criticism considers that the earliest testimony, including papyri, uncials, miniscules, and Sinaiticus support the Nestle-Aland 27 reading.

28. Augustine, *On Christian Doctrine*, 4.

29. Ibid., 65.

30. Ibid., 109.

31. Tan, *Interpretation of Prophecy*, 109.

32. Ibid., 110.

economies in the outworking of God's purpose and which sees the ultimate purpose of God to bring glory to himself in all his relations with all his creatures."[33] Charles Ryrie identifies the *sine qua non*[34] of dispensational theology as including three elements: the consistent application of the literal grammatical-historical hermeneutic, the understanding that Israel and the church are distinct (the church does not replace Israel, and thereby does not fulfill the promises of future blessing made to the nation of Israel), and the understanding that the underlying purpose of God in the world is his own glory.[35] The key distinguishing mark of dispensational theology, according to Ryrie, is its commitment to the *consistent* application of the literal hermeneutic. The other two aspects arguably result from that prior methodological commitment.

Covenant theologian John Gerstner illustrates the hermeneutic distinctions between dispensational and covenant theology in his chastisement of dispensationalism: "The non-dispensationalist tends, in his view, to be more sophisticated and less submissive while dispensationalists . . . 'tremble' more at God's Word. This conviction . . . can lead to a spiritual arrogance . . . Thinking that they see the truth clearly . . . By a certain naiveté they suppose that their method brings them into an immediate apprehension of Scripture as over against the 'interpretations' of others."[36] Gerstner further represents the foundational difference between dispensationalism and covenant theology as a subtle hermeneutic point: "We all are literalists up to a certain point. At the point where we differ, there is a tendency for the dispensationalists to be literalistic where the non-dispensationalist tends to interpret the Bible figuratively."[37] The greatest area of difference between the two traditions is in the area of biblical prophecy.[38]

The recent developing progressive dispensationalism represents a third, mediating tradition.[39] As the name implies, literal grammatical-historical is the starting point, but proponents perceive a deficiency in dispensational theology that needs *progressing*. Dispensationalism

33. Lightner, *Handbook of Evangelical Theology*, 240.

34. Latin, *without which not*.

35. Ryrie, *Dispensationalism Today*, 44–46.

36. Gerstner, *Wrongly Dividing the Word*, 91.

37. Ibid., 93.

38. For example Berkhof, *Systematic Theology*, 712–14.

39. Saucy, *Case for Progressive Dispensationalism*, 27.

observes the primacy of the Hebrew Bible in matters of definition, whereas progressive dispensationalism suggests that the Greek New Testament is primary when it comes to defining words and concepts.[40] Progressive dispensationalism "seeks to retain a natural understanding of the prophetic Scriptures,"[41] but it acknowledges that New Testament expansions of promises made in the Old Testament are representative of a "complementary principle"[42] that characterizes the New Testament use of the Old. Blaising and Bock, two of the founders of progressive dispensationalism, suggest that this is not a departure from literal interpretation in favor of allegorical interpretation, but rather that "progressive dispensationalism is a development of 'literal' interpretation into a more consistent historical-literary interpretation."[43]

Each of these three traditions affirms literal hermeneutics as a core value, yet the three disagree on subtle nuances in application (of course, the distinctions are profound in application and result). It is notable, for the sake of the present discussion, that despite differences in interpreting predictive prophecy, the three traditions generally agree on the handling of Genesis 1–11 (that it is intended as literal and propositional), which is the central section of the Bible at stake in critiques by Leopold, McHarg, and White. Thus while there are distinctive groups within the EC, the level of consistency among the three groups in interpreting Genesis 1–11 as literal and propositional allows for the EC to be considered as a whole, for purposes of the present discussion. That is not to say that differences do not exist—some of those distinctions are highlighted in forthcoming sections—rather it is to say that the underlying principles of biblical authority and hermeneutic methodology, to which the EC submits, require the EC to reject the basic premises of Leopold's, McHarg's and White's rejection of the creationist worldview in Genesis. Considering that as recently as 2008 some 34 percent of adults in the U. S. "considered themselves Born Again or Evangelical Christians, this is not a demographic that can be ignored."[44] Is it possible, then, to reframe the critiques in a way that the EC can receive and positively respond to them, without

40. While interlocutors must consider texts in diverse languages (Hebrew, Aramaic, and Greek), the Greek Septuagint is often helpful in demonstrating equivalent concepts in translation from Hebrew to Greek.

41. Ibid.

42. Blaising and Bock, *Progressive Dispensationalism*, 103.

43. Ibid., 52.

44. Kosmin and Keysar, *American Religious Identification*, 9.

demanding an abandonment of the EC's own defining principles? To propose just such a reframing is the aim of this book.

3

Four Interpretations of the Early Genesis Narrative

As clarity has increased in recent years regarding at least some aspects of the environmental consequences of ecologically insensitive human behavior, the chasm between fundamental aspects of the EC and the environmental movement has not narrowed. Early critiques of the biblical worldview and its ecological ramifications by the intellectual founders of the environmental movement were not particularly well informed, nor were they aimed with any degree of precision. Consequently, they served to have little effect in the EC beyond further alienating a significant percentage of the American populous from the environmental movement as it is typically defined. That is not to say that there have not been attempts by the EC to counter the critiques and to try to close the gap. In fact, there have been efforts within and without the EC to remove some if not all of the blame from the biblical worldview.

At issue is primarily the dominion mandate of Genesis 1:26–28:

> Then God said, "Let Us make man in Our image, according to Our likeness; and let them rule over the fish of the sea and over the birds of the sky and over the cattle, and over every creeping thing that creeps on the earth." And God created man in His own image, in the image of God He created him; male and female He created them. And God blessed them; and God said to them, "Be fruitful and multiply, and fill the earth, and subdue

> it; and rule over the fish of the sea and over the birds of the sky, and over every living thing that moves on the earth."

Leopold, McHarg, and White assume what may be called the despotic interpretation or dominionism. The two terms are equivalent, and used by different commentators to reference the same idea—that man was given a lasting dominion that places mankind over nature, and for his own purposes. It is fair to say that biblical interpreters, even from antiquity, did not see this interpretation as either problematic, or as needing reassessing. Only in recent years, as environmental considerations have moved into public focus, has this interpretation come to be viewed by some as inadequate. As a result several other interpretive approaches besides dominionism have been employed. In particular, the following section considers the stewardship interpretation, the citizenship model, and redacted dominionism (the preferred model proposed in this project) in comparison to dominionism.

In light of the EC's hermeneutic standard, dominionism (or despotism) relies on a literal grammatical-historical hermeneutic for its initial descriptions, understanding the rule and subdue imperatives to indicate just that: rule and subdue. However, the dominionist understanding fails the consistency test, as it infers a *theological* principle with universal implications: that man's ontological and functional value is established in Genesis 1:26–28 and is not altered thereafter. To maintain this theological premise requires the application of a theological (rather than literal) hermeneutic to the postdiluvian cultural mandate of Genesis 9:7—specifically, in that the dominion mandate is read into the postdiluvian cultural mandate which seems to deliberately omit the details of the dominion mandate that appeared in 1:26–28. In short, if one were to examine the postdiluvian context exclusively, there would be no reason whatsoever to conclude that man was to exercise any sovereignty over nature. Only by reading the previous conditions into the latter passages can one derive a continued dominion mandate. Thus, the fountainhead of the dominionist interpretation is, at least for the EC, an unjustifiably inconsistent hermeneutic, by the EC's own standards.

These early chapters are clearly vital to the EC worldview, and White's proposals—well intentioned though they may be—are unacceptable to the EC, as they require an admission that Genesis 1–2 is quite fallible. One reason to think they are fallible is because they contain two accounts of creation that appear to be mutually contradictory. If so, both accounts cannot be true and thus Genesis 1–2 is fallible. The EC, however, perceives no contradiction or inconsistency whatsoever in Genesis 1–2. Eugene Merrill, Distinguished Professor of Old Testament Studies at a prominent evangelical seminary, argues against any contradiction between the two creation accounts. He observes,

> Bible students have long noted the two records of creation . . . Historical-critical analysis has typically viewed these as coming from two originally independent sources . . . Such thinking shows abysmal insensitivity to the theological differences of the names Elohim and Yahweh, and the cosmological (or cosmocentric) nature of the first chapter as opposed to the anthropocentric nature of the second chapter. Furthermore, it is being seriously challenged by recent literary-rhetorical approaches that make a case for unity of composition by a common author. The two creation texts are thus to be seen not as competing, but as complementary—viewing the event from two different angles.[1]

Merrill counters the contradiction accusation on structural and thematic grounds, and he adds, "There is a perfectly good theological reason why Genesis should contain two creation accounts and why the first account has one divine name and the second has the other."[2] EC scholars also consider textual details such as the use of the ordinals preceding the term יום (*yom*, translated *day*) in Genesis 1, while noting that the ordinal is not associated with the term in the second account, allowing that the term *day* is being used differently in the two contexts. As for the theological differences in divine terms to which Merrill alludes, Exodus 6:2–3 illustrates a distinction between אלוהים (*elohim*) as a title for God, and יהוה (*Yahweh*) as the proper name of God. From this context, the text indicates that God revealed himself initially by his title, whereas he would later be known to Israel by his proper name, as he was to Moses.

From an EC perspective, the employment of the two different terms in the early Genesis account implies different relationships and emphasizes different perspectives. These differences (along with syntactical keys, such as singular and plural pronouns, etc.) help to clarify the Genesis 1 account as anticipating the creation of mankind collectively, whereas Genesis 2 tightens focus on a specific man and woman and God's intimate relationship with them. Incidentally, as the discussion vacillates

1. Merrill, "Genesis 1–11 as Literal History," 85.

2. Ibid., 87.

between *man* collectively and *Adam* specifically in the following pages, both syntactical aspects and conceptual elements contribute to clarity regarding the actual referent of the texts addressed, because the same Hebrew word is used for both in the early Genesis narrative. In any case, Merrill's comments illustrate the EC's general unwillingness to make any concessions of inconsistency in the first two chapters of Genesis.[3]

In light of environmental concerns raised by the despotic interpretation, biblical interpreters within and without the EC have considered a second interpretive model that redefines *dominion* as *stewardship*, interpreting the dominion mandate of 1:26–28 in light of a perceived stewardship description found in Genesis 2.[4] Considered in light of the EC interpretive method, the stewardship interpretation seems itself to be a hermeneutic contradiction.

First, it follows from a metaphorical interpretation of the rule and subdue mandate. Only if one were to argue that the creation narratives were metaphorical in their entirety could one justify understanding the mandate as figurative. Yet, EC adherents to the stewardship interpretation do not view the narrative as metaphoric (and thus face inconsistency accusations).[5] Further, if the narratives are purely metaphorical, then metaphysical distinctions between man and nature are virtually unjustifiable, as the intended referents of the figurative language are far less than certain. Second, the stewardship interpretation does not consider the progress of the narrative, and makes no allowance for the condition changes resulting from the Fall. Finally, as in the despotic interpretation, the theological hermeneutic is applied to Genesis 9:7 to read the dominion (albeit redefined) mandate into the text. Although the stewardship is the most ecologically friendly of the two common interpretations, it also requires a high degree of inconsistency for its derivation. Although the stewardship interpretation is the most commonly represented by writers in the EC, it does not overcome the early critiques of the environmental movement, because anthropocentrism and human sovereignty over nature remain important factors in the equation. Stewardship, then, neither

3. The issue of agreement between Genesis 1 and 2 are given a more thorough treatment in the exegetical section of this present project.

4. Specifically 2:15: "Then the Lord God took the man and put him into the garden of Eden to cultivate it and keep it." As there is no mention here of dominion, specifically, the majority interpretation of the EC at present is that the dominion of Genesis 1 is equivalent to the cultivating and keeping of Genesis 2.

5. For example Terry, *Biblical Hermeneutics*, 551; and Morris, *Genesis Record*, 92.

resolves the issues at hand, nor does it consistently apply hermeneutic principles readily accepted by the EC.

Callicott, perhaps with some sympathy for those wrestling clumsily with these passages to no avail, proposes what he calls the citizenship interpretation, in which man is designed to be considerate co-citizen with all other aspects of nature, and that "anthropocentrism itself is man's original sin and is responsible for the famous Fall."[6] Considered in light of EC methodology, the citizenship interpretation is appealing in one respect, from the point of view of a literal grammatical-historical approach, in that it considers the progress of the narrative in a sequential manner. However, it also leans heavily on a metaphoric interpretation in that it considers the narrative as mythic. Consequently the interpretation infers spiritual truths beyond the propositions present in the text. Further, it does not seem to account for the dominion mandate as representing a pre-Fall human sovereignty over nature. While citizenship offers the highest degree of consistency with an evolutionary-ecological worldview of the three interpretations, divergent hermeneutic approaches in its derivation renders it virtually untenable for application in the EC.

A fourth interpretive model, here identified as *redacted dominionism,* and proposed by this writer to be the best evangelical reading of the text, is an attempt at applying a consistent literal grammatical-historical hermeneutic to the entire early Genesis narrative. It considers the *rule* and *subdue* imperative in its most natural lexical sense, recognizes the condition changes brought by the Fall, and recognizes the delicate textual distinctions between the pre-Fall and post-Fall cultural mandates. Further, redacted dominionism avoids the metaphorical reliance that poison the stewardship and citizenship views, and it eschews the theological eisegesis to which the despotic dominionism view succumbs.

Redacted dominionism is the only of the four interpretations (the others being despotism, stewardship, and citizenship) that claims consistent application of the literal grammatical-historical hermeneutic in accordance with EC methodology, and resulting from this method it is the only one of the four that supports the universal instrumental value of all created things—a value model proposed in forthcoming discussions as grounding equality of human and nonhuman beings. Besides allowing for the highest degree of textual integrity in light of EC methodology, the literal grammatical-historical method is advantageous in this context as

6. Callicott, *Earth's Insights*, 19.

its consistent use allows for the total immunity of the early Genesis narrative from the critiques levied against it by Leopold, McHarg, and White.

The crux of White's assessment, for example, is that the Judeo-Christian tradition fosters anthropocentrism, yet redacted dominionism results in a doxological rather than anthropocentric model, recognizing that all things exist to glorify God, and this function is not a responsibility only of humanity (e.g., see Ps 19:1). Being doxological and decidedly nonanthropocentric, redacted dominionism asserts that all creatures have only instrumental value as determined by their creator. As such, human and nonhuman beings share the same kind of value, and simply express that valuation within varying roles (functions) defined by the creator.

If we are to discover an interpretation that can be viewed as valid in the EC for the purposes of grounding an environmental ethic that is both comprehensive and equitable for all creatures, it seems the interpretation must meet at least the following criteria: (1) it must be justifiable from the text itself, (2) it ought to maintain the highest degree of textual integrity in applying EC methodology, (3) ideally, it should represent human and nonhuman beings as having equal value, and (4) consequently it represents the strongest possible biblical environmental ethic because it does not derive from an anthropocentric theology, and it avoids a value hierarchy within the creation. It will be argued here that redacted dominionism is the only one of the four readings of Genesis considered here that meets each of these qualifications: (1) it is derived directly from the text and by no extraordinary effort—no "text torturing"—beyond the application of EC methodology in the exegetical process, (2) it may be seen from the EC vantage point as maintaining the greatest level of hermeneutic consistency of the four interpretations,[7] (3) it represents all human and nonhuman creatures as having equal instrumental (specifically doxological) value to God, and (4) it depicts a doxological—and nonanthropocentric—teleology. In short, the argument to be made here is that redacted dominionism, as an alternative fourth interpretive model, offers, within evangelical methodology, an environmentally sympathetic reading of the early Genesis narrative and provides a plausible basis within the evangelical community for a biblical environmental ethic.

7. Despotism, stewardship, citizenship, and redacted dominionism.

4

Framing the Argument

LYNN WHITE SUMMARIZES HIS critique of Western environmental attitudes in saying that they are primarily "shaped by the Judeo-Christian dogma of creation."[1] In particular, he makes seven claims regarding implications of Genesis that are particularly relevant to environmental ethics: (1) that God planned all of this explicitly for man's benefit and rule; (2) that no item in the physical creation had any purpose save to serve man's purposes; (3) that Christianity is the most anthropocentric religion the world has seen; (4) that man shares, in great measure, God's transcendence of nature; (5) that it is God's will that man exploit nature for his proper ends, and that Christianity made it possible to exploit nature in a mood of indifference to the feelings of natural objects; (6) that man's effective monopoly on spirit in this world was confirmed by Christianity, and consequently the old pagan inhibitions to the exploitation of nature crumbled; and (7) that man's transcendence of and rightful mastery over nature is a Christian dogma.[2] Chapter 2 examines these claims, providing a vehicle for introduction to some of the challenges that an evangelical reading of Genesis must address if it is to be perceived by those outside the EC as being at all relevant to discussion of environmental concerns.

Whereas the central issue of White's claims is that Christianity is inherently anthropocentric, this claim is only problematic for White because he asserts that we will not resolve the present ecological crisis "until

1. White, "Historical Roots," 1206.

2. Ibid., 1203–7.

we find a new religion, or rethink our old one."[3] By "new," presumably White means a nonanthropocentric one. Recall that his first suggestion is not an option for the EC, and his second comes with a proposal—biblically unjustified Franciscan theology—equally unacceptable to the EC. He characterizes beliefs about our nature and destiny as religion, and particularly describes the "axiom that nature has no reason for existence save to serve man" as distinctively Christian.[4] White's anthropocentric indictment of Christianity on grounds of alleged anthropocentrism is not nuanced enough, as it stands, to be answered with precision.

Finally, White and other critics have perceived that Genesis promotes intrinsic value only for human beings and strictly instrumental value for all things nonhuman.[5] Cal DeWitt, by contrast, understands Genesis[6] to affirm the intrinsic value to all created things.[7] Callicott views this as at least somewhat advantageous,[8] and further considers that Genesis may indeed be understood to promote intrinsic value of nonhuman things, though he acknowledges both views are textually plausible.[9] Chapter 2 concludes with a consideration of intrinsic and instrumental value, as the forthcoming handling of Genesis pivots on the distinction between the two.

Chapter 3 considers pertinent passages in the early Genesis narrative, first, in order to show the groundings of the four major interpretive views (dominionism, stewardship, citizenship, and redacted dominionism), and additionally to show how arguments such as White's may be countered within the context of an EC reading of the text. The discussion commences with an evangelical reading of relevant aspects of Genesis 1–2, beginning with a discussion of Genesis 1:26–28, a passage generally interpreted as asserting one of two views regarding the role of humanity

3. Ibid., 1206.

4. Ibid., 1207.

5. White, "Historical Roots," 1205, 1207; and critics such as Fortin, "Bible Made Me Do It," 199.

6. By way of the stewardship interpretation of Genesis 1:26–28.

7. A few samples include DeWitt, in his support of what he calls "deep stewardship." DeWitt, "Behemoth and Batrachians," 291–316. See also Bullmore, "Four Most Important Biblical Passages," 158; Rogerson, *Genesis 1–11*, 19; and Rosenberg, "Concepts of Torah and Nature," 219.

8. Callicott "Non-Anthropocentric Value Theory," 302.

9. For example Callicott, *Defense of the Land Ethic*, 137, 138.

in the universe (on the one hand, despotism or dominionism,[10] and on the other, stewardship[11]). Two other possible interpretations (citizenship[12] and redacted dominionism) are considered. Callicott's citizenship approach anticipates the Fall in Genesis 3 and recognizes an adjustment in the trajectory of the early mandate. It is worth noting that Rashi, Ross, Sacks, Morris, and Rosenberg, etc., similarly anticipate the Genesis 3 events and their effect on the man/nature relationship,[13] so this contribution of the citizenship interpretation is not a novel consideration, but its rejection of the legitimacy of Genesis 1 makes it incompatible with EC interpretive method. A fourth view proposed here, redacted dominionism, likewise accounts for the events of Genesis 3, but considers those events especially in light of the redacted dominion mandate of 9:7.

As the Genesis texts are handled here in sequential and exegetical fashion through an EC lens, White's allegations are also considered as the Genesis account warrants. One such claim is related to Adam's relationship to the rest of creation. Adam is named after the dirt from which he is made (cf. 1:26 and 2:7). This is inferred by the EC to suggest that man is a part of nature, rather than transcendent over it. This is the first step in the textual case against White's assertion that "man shares, in great measure, God's transcendence of nature."[14] Further steps are considered in examination of Genesis 1:26–28; 3:1–19; 6:5–12; 9:1–17, and Psalm 8:4–8 collectively.

Man (understood in an EC reading as referring to mankind collectively because plural pronouns and verbs are employed in the description of human essence and activities) is made in the *imago Dei*, or image of God (Gen 1:26). As a direct result of this ontological distinction from the rest of nature, Adam (understood in an EC reading as referring to the first created man because singular pronouns and verbs are employed in description of his essence and activities), in his initial and perfect state,

10. For example McHarg, "Place of Nature," 1–12; Hiebert, "Human Vocation," 138; Jamieson et al, *Commentary*, 8; and Poole, *Commentary on the Holy Bible*, 4.

11. For example Morris, *Genesis Record*, 77; DeWitt, "Behemoth and Batrachians," 291–316; Bullmore, "Four Most Important Biblical Passages," 158; Rogerson, *Genesis 1–11*, 19; and Rosenberg, "Concepts of Torah and Nature," 219.

12. Callicott, *Earth's Insights*, 19.

13. For example Sacks, *Lion and the Ass*, 46; Ross, "Genesis," 29; Ben Isaiah and Sharfman, *Pentateuch and Rashi's Commentary*, 14; Morris, *Genesis Record*, 77; and Rosenberg, "Concepts of Torah and Nature," 219.

14. White, "Historical Roots," 1205.

was evidently expected to rule or have dominion over the earth and all other living things (cf. 1:26 and 1:28). Importantly, the *imago Dei* is the only reason given for the dominion mandate; thus if there is later adjustment to human identity and qualification pertaining to the *imago Dei* (as there appears to be in Genesis 3), then it would not be surprising that the dominion mandate might be adjusted. That the mandate may have been adjusted in such a manner is considered at length in the following discussion of Genesis 3 and 8:15—9:7.

Of further note in the context of man's creation, is that there is no indication of God's intended purpose for creating man, outside of the consistent de-emphasis of man's purposes and plans, and the emphasis of God's purposes and plans (e.g., 1:26; 2:5, 15–16, 18–19; 3:14, 17–19; 6:3, 6–7, 13, 22; 8:21–22). White's allegation that "no item in the physical creation had any purpose save to serve man's purposes" has no basis in "the Judeo-Christian dogma of creation," and seems even to be contradicted by it.[15] Chapter 3 concludes with a discussion of humanity being told to be fruitful and multiply and fill the earth (Gen 1:28). In light of the imperatives to fill the whole earth, there may be early restrictions on human conduct that further agree with a redacted dominionism interpretation, and that may even begin to challenge White's assertion that Christianity is the world's most anthropocentric religion.[16]

That the sin of Genesis 3 resulted in a changed condition for man and all creation (3:14–19) is a point of emphasis in chapter 4 (a continuation of the EC reading of the early Genesis narrative to further underscore the grounding of the four interpretive views, and to answer White's critiques). First addressed is the significance of value theory in the early Genesis narrative, with particular emphasis on the ramifications of intrinsic and instrumental value. Here it is argued that intrinsic value is not the necessary condition for a nonanthropocentric environmental ethic, and that recognizing a comprehensive instrumental value of all created things may prove advantageous in the development of a biblical environmental ethic.

Further, as the glory of God is a focal point for the biblical writers, there is need of definition and consideration of what exactly the glory of God means, and how it relates to his purpose in creating and working within his creation, and how that purpose may be viewed as a vital

15. Ibid., 1205, 1207.

16. Ibid., 1205.

component of a nonanthropocentric environmental ethic. This discussion sets the necessary groundwork for the forthcoming consideration of passages relevant to the fall of creation in Genesis 3–9. These passages present a significant challenge to the dominionist interpretive model, in that they do not seem to allow for any human capability in keeping the dominion mandate. Consequently, man's dominion was a failure resulting in a curse for all creation, and Adam's labors in working with the earth would be, as a result, increasingly difficult (3:17). Adam would have a finite lifespan that would further inhibit discovery of and fruitfulness in nature (3:19).

Still, the most significant cost of sin was the tarnishing of the *imago Dei*, and its augmentation of a new image of Adam.[17] This ontological change came with a pronouncement contrasting the Genesis 1:31 declaration that it was all "very good." Instead, "the Lord saw that the wickedness of man was great on the earth and that every intent of the thoughts of his heart was only evil continually" (6:5). The downward spiral evident in Genesis 1–11 differs substantially from White's claim that "implicit faith in perpetual progress . . . is rooted in and indefensible apart from Judeo-Christian teleology."[18] While amillennial and postmillennial interpretations have historically held to the idea of implicit faith in perpetual progress, premillennialism (a prominent interpretation in the EC) rejects the idea, recognizing that despite efforts mandated by various biblical ethics, the world will not progress toward a golden age without divine intervention.

The retribution of 6:13—that man was to be destroyed with the other creatures—shows a decidedly nonanthropocentric and indeed a theocentric perspective exercised by God.[19] Further, it counters White's claim that it is God's will that man exploit nature for his proper ends, and that Christianity made it possible to exploit nature in a mood of indifference to the feelings of natural objects. Man was not to exploit nature, but was a part of it, and was judged, in part, based on his failure to live in consideration of nature (3:24). Further, Genesis 7:15 describes all living things as having the breath (spirit) of life. White's diagnosis that "man's

17. Genesis 5:3 indicates that the son of Adam was made in Adam's image, in contrast to the *imago Dei* possessed at least initially by Adam.

18. White, "Historical Roots," 1205.

19. Whereas the term *doxological* addresses the end to which all things are working in this EC reading, the term *theocentric* addresses the central person as God rather than man, as would be the central figure in an *anthropocentric* understanding.

effective monopoly on spirit in this world was confirmed by Christianity," is countered by an evangelical reading of the textual evidence in this context.[20]

After the judgment of Genesis 6–8, humanity was to go out with the same simple purpose as that of all other living things: proliferation (8:17). Post-Fall conditions are not repaired to pre-Fall glory (8:21). In order for humanity to even survive, special accommodations are introduced, including a prohibition of murder (9:6), and the fear of man in animals (9:2, 5). No longer is man qualified or equipped to dominate, or even to steward, thus the dominion and stewardship interpretations are challenged in resolving tensions between the dominion mandate of 1:26–28 and the redacted mandates of 8:15—9:7. Most notably, 9:7 repeats verbatim the mandate of 1:28 in all respects with the exception of the dominion aspect. This challenges White's allegation that "man's transcendence of and rightful mastery over nature" is a Christian dogma.[21]

The accommodations made in 8:15—9:7 and the universal aspects discussed in 9:12–16[22] indicate that contrary to White's assertion, that God did not plan all of nature explicitly for man's benefit and rule, but rather for his own. Further, this context disputes White's observation that "it is God's will that man exploit nature for his proper ends,"[23] on the grounds that God actively places limits on his own and on human activity in order for the continual existence and function of nature (cf. 8:21 and 9:4). In light of the broad context of the early Genesis narratives, White's accusation that "Christianity is the most anthropocentric religion the world has seen" is too broad, and may even be countered by theocentric themes in Genesis 1–11.[24]

The exegetical material of chapter 4 concludes with a discussion of an important complementary passage to the Genesis account. Psalm 8:4–8 is one of the most controversial passages considering human and nonhuman value, being often understood by Judaic and Christian interpreters to be asserting human sovereignty over nature.[25] A brief

20. White, "Historical Roots," 1206.

21. Ibid.

22. The covenant is repeatedly referenced as being made not just with humanity, but also with every living creature.

23. White, "Historical Roots," 1205.

24. Ibid.

25. For example A. Cohen, *Psalms*, 19; F. Gaebelein, *Expositor's Bible Commentary*, 114; and Keil and Delitzsch, *Commentary on the Old Testament*, 5:94.

exegetical examination of the Hebrew grammar utilized in the passage supports two other possible interpretations: (1) that the passage speaks prophetically and is not describing current conditions, and (2) that the passage is not speaking generally about humanity, but rather is speaking specifically of one man. The writer of Hebrews quotes the passage as if to favor the latter (Heb 2:5–9). David Werther introduces an additional logical point regarding ontological and functional superiority that contradicts the *humanity as presently sovereign* interpretation.[26] If Werther or either of the alternative grammatical scenarios is correct, then the redacted dominionism interpretation of Genesis is consistent with even the most troublesome value passage outside of Genesis.

These passages, considered with earlier and related contexts and from the vantage point of an evangelical reading, may be understood to support what this project terms *redacted dominionism*. This interpretation of the early Genesis narrative and related contexts proposes a biblical environmental ethic that is theocentric rather than anthropocentric in its explanation for the existence and function of all created things, human and nonhuman, an environmental ethic that is based on the instrumental rather than intrinsic value of all created things, an environmental ethic that is more compatible with EC hermeneutic methodology than dominionism (or the despotic interpretation), stewardship, or citizenship. Finally, it proposes an environmental ethic that provides an answer to White's critiques that Christianity is inherently anthropocentric, and an environmental ethic that, consequently, may be a helpful device for those within and without the evangelical community.

26. Werther, "Reason and the Imago Dei," 327.

5

Lynn White's Seven Claims Regarding the Genesis Narrative

As White's comments have been particularly influential in setting the agenda for environmental considerations during the past nearly fifty years, it is not unreasonable to expect that an evangelical environmental ethic should be able to answer White's allegations against Western interpretations of the early Genesis narrative. This chapter discusses with specificity the implications of White's most significant points.

While White's claims are diverse in their subject matter and scope, they are ordered here as they appear in White's paper, rather than systematized in topical fashion. Similarly, in the forthcoming consideration of the text of Genesis, concepts and ideas are handled as they appear in the text. This method is prioritized within the EC to allow the text itself, at least to some degree, to set the course of the discussion. Handling White's "Historical Roots" in this fashion, seven distinct claims relevant to environmental ethics regarding the implications of the Genesis dogma of creation are discernible: (1) that God planned all of this explicitly for man's benefit and rule; (2) that no item in the physical creation had any purpose save to serve man's purposes; (3) that Christianity is the most anthropocentric religion the world has seen; (4) that man shares, in great measure, God's transcendence of nature; (5) that it is God's will that man exploit nature for his proper ends, and that Christianity made it possible to exploit nature in a mood of indifference to the feelings of natural objects; (6) that man's effective monopoly on spirit in this world was confirmed by Christianity, and consequently the old pagan inhibitions to the exploitation of nature crumbled; and (7) that man's transcendence of and rightful mastery over nature is a Christian dogma.[1]

(1) "God planned all of this explicitly for man's benefit and rule"[2]

White's avouchment of God's intentionality adds a theological component to his textual challenge. As it is, White seems to be representing the Western interpretation as promoting a divinely inspired anthropocentric teleology, but as White is a theist arguing against an anthropocentric worldview, he seems quite unconvinced of the adequacy of the Genesis teleology as he considers it here. Still, White asseverates that a plan to an anthropocentric end is explicit in the dominant Western interpretation of the Genesis text. White seems to take this claim for granted, offering no particular evidence; still, the claim is made, and is worthy of a response because of its resonance with much of Christian history and its impact on subsequent environmental scholarship.

Logical tensions and absence of evidence aside, the teleology White puts forth is first for man's benefit, and second for his rule (though admittedly, it is unclear to this writer if the order has any significance to White). This sounds remarkably like the teleological model of Francis Bacon's *New Atlantis*: God is glorified by human discovery (and mastery, to use Descartes's term) of nature and the fruit of said discovery benefits humanity.[3] While it is clear that the man-centered schema is not White's own invention, one might justifiably wonder whether the anthropocentric design White alleges is explicit in the Genesis account, as White claims, or whether it is grounded in other influential sources (such as Bacon and Descartes, that White mentions only in brief).

1. White, "Historical Roots," 1203–7.
2. Ibid., 1205.
3. Bacon, *New Atlantis*, 170–71.

(2) "No item in the physical creation had any purpose save to serve man's purposes"[4]

Despite the availability of second-century testimony agreeable to White's allegation,[5] he does not allude to extra-canonical theology to support his third and fourth claim, but rather he includes this allegation of anthropocentrism as the representation of the creation story itself. While White's previous claim centered on teleology, this one is more categorical in its scope, being perhaps the most hyperbolic of White's claims. Without some explicit statement in Genesis about physical creation only serving man's purposes, or at least a citation of early testimony supporting his anthropocentric interpretation, his claim stands unjustified. Still, an evangelical environmental ethic should answer this charge—if not as directly related to the Genesis account, then as a definitive point leading either to anthropocentrism or to a more environmentally considerate (and less anthropocentric) conclusion.

In making this claim White assumes distinct boundaries of a physical/spiritual duality in creation. In his earlier statement that "man and nature are two things, and man is master," White implies two separate categories of things.[6] He builds on his premise that God planned this explicitly for man's benefit and rule, and undergirds a later claim that man has a monopoly on spirit. By characterizing the remainder of creation as physical and acknowledging spirituality as uniquely human, White's critique extends beyond the mere teleological statement that he enunciates. It speaks of more than mere purpose and function; rather it is a statement of essential identity. In his suggestion that humanity is uniquely endowed with both spirit and body, White takes for granted that the non-spiritual would then be subject to the spiritual as a result.

For illustration, consider the following argument derived from White's assertion:

> Premise 1: Humans are ontologically superior to the nonhuman creation.
>
> Premise 2: Functional superiority is derived from ontological superiority.

4. White, "Historical Roots" 1205.

5. For example, "All things, as we teach, were created by God, and given to man for his use," and "it is man's by free gift of its maker." Tertullian, *De Spectaculis*, ch. 2.

6. White, "Historical Roots," 1205.

> Conclusion: Thus, humans have functional superiority over the nonhuman creation.

White implies that the first premise is found in Genesis. He observes that Christianity "established a dualism of man and nature," and promoted man's transcendence of nature.[7] Presumably, this transcendence is derived from man's possession of spirit by virtue of the *imago Dei*. The second premise is an assumed one. White does not defend this premise implicitly or otherwise, instead he takes it for granted. If one assumes the second premise, then the conclusion is not a difficult one at which to arrive. His interpretation of Genesis on this point succeeds based on the idea that ontological superiority demands functional superiority. His assumption is not an uncommon one, as assumptions (by other interpreters) to that effect are considered in the forthcoming discussion of Psalm 8 (discussed in chapter 4).

Still, White's interpretation of Genesis requires several pieces of evidence: (1) the creation story should make some statement, explicit or implicit, identifying a telos for the physical creation; (2) the creation story should identify that end as anthropocentric; further, (3) the creation story should define the man/nature dichotomy as White characterizes it; and finally, (4) the creation story should provide some direction regarding the relation between ontological and functional superiority. In an EC reading of the creation story, as discussed in the forthcoming handling of the early Genesis narrative, statements of purpose for creation may be understood as decidedly not anthropocentric. Consequently, White's strong man/nature dichotomy does not hold up, as Genesis, along with Psalm 8, clarifies through a series of value statements that ontological and functional superiority are two separate things altogether.

(3) "Christianity is the most anthropocentric religion the world has seen"[8]

Before making this point, White traces the influence of Christianity in its application of the Judeo creation story. By adding the qualifier, "especially in its Western form," he clarifies that the target here is that particular application of the text rather than White's interpretation of the text.[9] Still,

7. Ibid., 1205, 1206.

8. Ibid., 1205.

9. Ibid.

White appeals as evidence to Tertullian's and Irenaeus's theology of the *imago Dei* in humanity, and in so doing raises the issue once again of human ontological superiority over nature.

Tertullian avers that the human soul is "formed by the breathing of God, and not out of matter."[10] As such, humanity has special standing, even being made from clay, because "God wholly employed and absorbed in it—in His hand, His eye, His labour, His purpose, His wisdom, His providence, and above all, in His love, which was dictating the lineaments (of this creature)."[11] The human soul differs from material things in that it is both the work and image of God.[12] Irenaeus emphasizes that God formed man "with His own hands," presumably considering the verbiage of Genesis 2:7, and that the formation of man was from ingredients that were "purest and finest."[13] Humanity was not merely part of nature, for God "traced His own form on the formation," and the resulting being was not only divine in essence, but even divine in form.[14]

Though White appeals to secondary sources to justify his claim (though he does not clarify whether he cites them as important on their own merits or whether he is considering their broader influence on Western Christianity), his allusion to the ontological superiority of humanity over nature draws attention back to the creation story, and to his previous claim that the whole of creation was to serve man's purposes. White's direct indictment of Christianity and indirect criticism of Genesis invites an important question to be addressed from an EC reading of the text: *does the Genesis account present an anthropocentric view of the human/nature dichotomy?* If an EC reading of Genesis is unable to escape the anthropocentric conclusion, then the testimony of Tertullian and Irenaeus is immediately relevant. However, if an EC reading counters anthropocentrism, then White's appeal to second-century Christian writers does little beyond reminding interlocutors that second-century Christianity had indeed tended toward the anthropocentric.

While the latter would be sufficient to justify his broader claim regarding Western Christianity, still, if there is discovered to be no proper grounding of anthropocentrism in Genesis within an EC reading, then

10. Tertullian, *De Anima*, ch. 3.

11. Tertullian, *De Resurrectione Carnis*, ch. 6.

12. Tertullian, *De Spectaculis*, ch. 2.

13. Irenaeus, *Demonstration of the Apostolic Preaching*, 79.

14. Ibid.

the creation story may itself be exonerated of the charges White levies against it—that it is primarily culpable for the pervasive anthropocentrism that followed centuries later. Further, the project at hand is not to exonerate Western Christianity from White's claim, but rather to show that his claim is not justifiably applied to "the striking story of creation"[15] if it is interpreted in an EC reading.

(4) "Man shares, in great measure, God's transcendence of nature"[16]

Adding to the testimony of Tertullian and Irenaeus, this claim, for White, provides further support for the previous one (that Christianity is the most anthropocentric religion the world has seen). It represents a theological justification of the idea that "man and nature are two things, and man is master."[17] As it turns out, this is perhaps White's most important claim, because it asserts the primary causal factor of the human/nature dichotomy. In White's representation of (at least) Western interpretations of Genesis, the dichotomy is grounded almost solely upon humanity's transcendent nature by way of the *imago Dei*. If White is correct in this claim, then several of the others are justified as well—especially regarding the anthropocentric thrust of Christianity.

In referencing Tertullian and Irenaeus, White notes that both thinkers perceived that Adam in some way foreshadowed the later incarnation of Christ. White suspects that if there is such a foreshadowing, it serves as further evidence of human transcendence over nature. If after all, man was made in the image of God (who transcends nature, being its creator[18]), and later God took on the image of man, through Christ (who was considered by Tertullian and Irenaeus, to be God incarnate), then surely Adam, as the image of God and foreshadower of Christ, must himself transcend nature in at least some significant way. In short, because God allegedly put on human flesh, then human flesh is glorified above all other nature. Further, ontological superiority of humanity seems justified

15. White, "Historical Roots," 1205.

16. Ibid.

17. Ibid.

18. As Irenaeus says, "God is not ruler and Lord over the things of another, but over His own." Irenaeus, *Demonstration of the Apostolic Preaching*, 73.

to White in light of the functional superiority he perceives humanity to possess.

Tertullian does impute significance to the First Adam in light of the incarnation of the Second Adam. He describes Adam's observation regarding the woman and marriage as a prophetic reference to the relationship of Christ and the church. The two (man and woman, and Christ and the church) are one flesh.[19] Consequently, he recognizes that humanity does transcend nonhuman nature. Still, Tertullian, in a subtle but important move, differentiates between the human soul and spirit. He maintains "the soul to be breath and not the spirit, in the scriptural and distinctive sense of the spirit."[20] He defends his assertion by alluding to Genesis 2:7. He says, "God breathed on man's face the breath of life, and that man became a living soul, by means of which he was both to live and breathe; at the same time making a distinction between the spirit and the soul."[21] He perceives the spirit to be the eternal and non-corporeal part of the person, while the soul is simply the breath of life.

Tertullian thus parses the human spirit and soul, perceiving the spirit to be the divine spark in man that gives him a transcendent nature. He further distinguishes between the spirit of God and the breath of God, suggesting "the spirit neither of God nor of the devil is naturally planted with a man's soul at his birth."[22] In observing this distinction, Tertullian would not assent fully with White's claim here. Tertullian clearly recognizes human transcendence, but not so far as to say that man shares God's transcendence. In short, Tertullian opines that man has the breath of life (soul), and additionally by virtue of possessing spirit, transcends nature, but he does not have (by natural means at creation or birth) the spirit of God, and thus he does not share God's unique kind of transcendence over nature.

Irenaeus likewise suggests that the First Adam prefigured the Second Adam: "For He made man the image of God; and the image of God is the Son, after whose image man was made: and for this cause He appeared in the end of the times that He might show the image (to be) like unto Himself."[23] Irenaeus's reference to the end of times may be of significance,

19. Tertullian, *De Anima*, ch. 11.

20. Ibid.

21. Ibid.

22. Ibid.

23. Irenaeus, *Demonstration of the Apostolic Preaching*, 90.

insofar as he understands that God and man did not share flesh until the incarnation. Thus any shared transcendence of nature between God and man would presumably not have been fully in place until the incarnation of Christ, at which time "He united man with God, and established a community of union between God and man."[24] Further, divine and human are said to share flesh—not spirit; so, Irenaeus discusses the connection of Christ to Adam not as human ascent, but rather as divine descent. If then there was no shared transcendence (between God and humanity) at creation, and at the incarnation God descended by taking on human flesh, then perhaps Irenaeus can be better represented as supporting the idea that God shares man's unity with nature rather than White's assertion that man shares, in great measure, God's transcendence of nature.

It seems, then, that the particular sources (Tertullian and Irenaeus) on which White relies do not adequately support his claim. Still, there is the matter of the creation story itself. The questions at hand are (1) whether Genesis imputes to humanity transcendence over nature, and (2) whether that transcendence is of like kind to that which characterizes God's relationship to nature.

(5) "It is God's will that man exploit nature for his proper ends," and "Christianity made it possible to exploit nature in a mood of indifference to the feelings of natural objects"[25]

White does not support these claims by any appeal to new evidence. Presumably, White perceives his case as a cumulative one. Perhaps because he thinks that he has adequately shown his earlier claims to be warranted, White seems to sense no obligation to textually ground this one. The claim has two prongs, with the second following from the first: (1) it is God's will that man exploit nature for man's proper ends, and (2) Christianity made it possible to exploit nature in a mood of indifference to the feelings of natural objects.

White seems to take the first prong for granted. Seemingly alluding to his cumulative case, he reminds the reader that Christianity established a human/nature dichotomy. If he is correct in his earlier allegations, then White's point that God wills for humans to exploit nature may be warranted. But without offering any further substantiation, he asserts

24. Ibid., 97–98.

25. White, "Historical Roots," 1205.

that it is God's will for man to exploit nature. Because he does not appeal to secondary sources here, it seems he is returning his attention to the Genesis creation story. Or perhaps he is alluding to the earlier claims that God planned all of this explicitly for man's benefit and rule, and that nothing in the physical creation had any purpose but to serve man's ends. Whether he is focusing directly on the Genesis account or on logical conclusions derived from those earlier claims (which he represents as inferences from the Genesis narrative), the evidence for this claim must be found in Genesis. For White's assertion to be warranted, we should expect to find some data in Genesis that speaks to the will of God for the utilization of nature exclusively in the service of humanity's own ends.

The second prong of this claim is focused less on the creation story than on the behavior it inspires. White's implication here is that Christianity has de-spirited nature, imputing to nature merely instrumental value, while humanity enjoys intrinsic value (by way of the *imago Dei*). White describes this de-spiriting as the "victory of Christianity over paganism," and understands that it took place at "the level of the common people" (ibid., 1205). He contrasts paganism (with its guardian spirits of nature) with Christianity, which allegedly showed disregard for the well being of nonhuman natural entities. He finds the former to be more environmentally compatible, because pagan animism promoted more personal interaction with nature than did (at least) Western Christianity. In any case, White perceives Christianity to have served as a catalyst for a resounding shift that represented "the greatest psychic revolution in the history of our culture" (ibid.). Thus for White, both the (Western interpretation of the) creation story and its application are to blame.

(6) "Man's effective monopoly on spirit in this world was confirmed [by Christianity], and consequently the old inhibitions to the exploitation of nature crumbled"[26]

Following on the heels of the preceding indictment, this one describes with precision the theological device by which Christianity supposedly made uncaring exploitation of nature possible, and restates the logical conclusion of applying the device. First, White seems careful not to insist here that Christianity first proclaimed human monopoly on spirit. Instead, he notes that Christianity confirmed the monopoly. At first glance

26. White, "Historical Roots," 1206.

it is not evident whether he blames the Genesis creation account for promoting human monopoly on spirit or whether he is simply targeting Christianity as more broadly comprised.

White's following comments are helpful in making clear his perception that the former is centrally culpable. He admits, "When one speaks in such sweeping terms, a note of caution is in order" (ibid., 1206). In taking a cautionary step back, he acknowledges the complexity of Christianity. He considers distinctive traditions of East and West, noting, for example, that his comments are more indicative of Western Christianity, because the Greek East "seems to have produced no marked technological innovation after the late 7th century" (ibid.). He further contrasts the contemplativeness of the East with the hyperactivity of the West, ceding that "the implications of Christianity for the conquest of nature would emerge more easily in the Western atmosphere" (ibid.) Still, while White considers in this context the implications of Christianity, he distinguishes between the substance and the implications. He perceives that Western thought was grounded in Christian theology, and he identifies both the cause and the effect. The effect is the "dynamism of religious devotion" and the cause is "the Judeo-Christian dogma of creation" (ibid.).

White admits to speaking in sweeping terms, and it is superficially evident that he is decrying the Western application of Judeo-Christian ideas. Still, it is inescapable that in this context he makes clear delineation between text and application, yet he offers no redemption for the text (as an EC solution would require), but only for the application (e.g., if the West would think more like the East, that would be better; if Western Christianity could think more like paganism, that would be better). White goes so far as to laud Francis of Assisi as the embodiment of such redemptive ideas, but White offers no prescription regarding alleged theological premises of the creation story that undergird his claims thus far. Further, he describes Christian arrogance toward nature as "orthodox" (1207). It seems that White directly blames the creation story, even prescribing heretical (to use White's word) applications to offset the teleology it suggests.[27]

As for the theological device White cites, it is, simply put, a human/nature dichotomy presumably derived from the creation story.

27. Recall his earlier characterization of Marxism as Judeo-Christian (if heretically so). Further, he extols Francis of Assisi, but references him as heretical as well. White is apparently unconcerned with tensions that may arise between orthodoxy and orthopraxy.

While earlier he communicates this dichotomy in general terms as man and nature representing two distinct things, he is more precise here in describing the dichotomy as grounded in a human monopoly on spirit. He observes that "although man's body is made of clay, he is not simply part of nature: he is made in God's image" (1205). In White's representation of Christianity, the *imago Dei* is most (if not entirely) represented in the non-corporeal part of humanity, and as such is best characterized as spirit.

Though Tertullian and Irenaeus were careful in distinguishing between spirit and soul, White is (perhaps understandably) unconcerned with such theological niceties. Still, this lack of subtlety seems to facilitate White's idea that Western Christianity—and the creation account specifically—promotes non-corporeal significance as residing only in humanity. To illustrate, he says, "To a Christian a tree can be no more than a physical fact," in contrast to pagan animism, which might perceive a tree as having a guardian spirit (1206). That man is unique in his possession of spirit is a characteristically Christian idea, arising directly from the creation account. Thus, to answer White's claim here, the Genesis position on the human/nature dichotomy should be clarified. Specifically, the question should be addressed whether in an EC reading nonhuman nature is represented in Genesis as possessing something non-corporeal.

White has argued that Western Christianity fostered anthropocentric themes in its application of the Genesis creation story. If the first part of his claim is correct (that humanity has a monopoly on spirit), then the second part represents further support for his broader claim. Here he considers that old inhibitions (represented by pagan animism) against exploitation of nature were dissolved by the rise of Christian anthropocentrism. In addition to questioning the biblical support for White's claim that humanity has a monopoly on spirit, one might also wonder whether even the Western iteration of Christianity bears as much culpability as White implies for the rise of exploitive attitudes toward nature, or if there are other causal factors in play as well. Still, an evangelical environmental ethic would need to handle effectively White's allegations of a Christianity-derived human/nature dichotomy that would seem *prima facie* to be incompatible with environmental considerations.

(7) Man's transcendence of and rightful mastery over nature is a Christian dogma[28]

The cause and effect relationship of ontological superiority and functional superiority is again evident in White's seventh claim. By this point in his argument he has already established to his satisfaction that both aspects of the assertion are grounded in Genesis and have been applied accordingly especially in Western Christianity. With his theological (considering the creation story and what it teaches about humanity's relationship to his environment) and historical (considering the application of the theological principles by its adherents) tasks assumed to be complete, this claim represents the capstone of his argument.

Leading up to this climax, White has already addressed the issue of human transcendence of nature with both theological and historical treatments. Further, he has also considered theological grounding for humanity's rightful mastery over nature. Still, he lends some attention to the history of how human functional superiority was applied. In a contrast of Eastern and Western Christianity, he recognizes that the Western iteration was more compatible with exploitive attitudes than was the Eastern permutation. He posits that Eastern Christianity was more inclined to perceive nature as revelatory of God and his character, and that "science as we conceive it could scarcely flourish in such an ambience" (ibid.). White illustrates his assertion by citing contrasting applications of natural theology, which was in the East "the decoding of the physical symbols of God's communication with man," but in the West became "the effort to understand God's mind by discovering how his creation operates" (Ibid.). White postulates that Western resolve to know the mind of God undergirded the further development of science, suggesting, "from the 13th century onward, up to and including Leibnitz and Newton, every major scientist, in effect, explained his motivations in religious terms" (ibid.).

In assessment of White's argument on this point it is fair to say that he attributes the rise of modern science and technology to ideas that are distinctively Christian—both in doctrine and in practice. It is noteworthy that he would make such a sweeping statement without invoking in this context the names of the two philosophical fathers of the modern scientific project—Bacon and Descartes. Such an omission invites further investigation to examine the connections between their motives and Christianity. Still, White admits, "It is often hard for the historian

28. Ibid.

to judge, when men explain why they are doing what they want to do, whether they are offering real reasons or merely culturally acceptable reasons" (ibid.). To his credit White acknowledges this difficulty, yet still he relies heavily—and in some cases, exclusively—upon such unreflective testimony to justify his argument. Even in appealing to the creation story to justify human transcendence of nature, he offers no textual evidence, instead assuming an interpretation that is clearly problematic and not often supported by early secondary evidence,[29] and citing adherents who seemingly applied the text according to certain aspects of said interpretation (e.g., Tertullian and Irenaeus).

While White's culminating claim, that man's transcendence of and rightful mastery over nature is a Christian dogma, first invites investigation of the textual evidence of the creation story to verify whether or not Genesis promotes human transcendence of nature and consequent human mastery of nature, it further invites examination of historical data, in particular, regarding whether or not Christianity was indeed the primary causal factor in the development of anthropocentric themes such as human mastery of nature in the context of the modern scientific project.

The coherence and grounding of White's indictments of Christianity are at times questionable. Still his claims have become clichés within the environmental movement, and as such represent important obstacles to be overcome by Bible-based environmental ethics. An evangelical environmental ethic, if it is to contribute positively in environmental matters, should be able to address at least the following of White's charges: that Genesis promotes faith in perpetual progress, and the connection between perpetual progress and positive or negative environmental attitudes or actions. Genesis describes an anthropocentric (and even androcentric) teleology, in which humanity is transcendent over nature, and in which nonhuman nature is intended only as a resource for humans. Human transcendence over nature is confirmed by similarities to God and dissimilarities to nonhuman things, and consequently humanity has historically asserted its mastery over nature in environmentally unsympathetic ways.

One measure of the usefulness of a Bible-based environmental ethic is how the ethic can handle White's allegations. Within an EC reading of the early Genesis narrative and associated passages, it will be argued here

29. For example, that Eve was an afterthought (and consequently not as important as Adam) is not at all a commonly held view, in part due to the logical tensions the assertion implies.

that of the four interpretive models discussed (dominionism, stewardship, citizenship, and redacted dominionism) redacted dominionism answers these charges with the highest degree of internal consistency. Thus White's diagnosis affords an opportunity to show the superiority of the redacted dominionism model over and against the other three, as core elements of each model are exposed in the light of White's challenges. Consequently, White's critique is an invaluable component of the present discussion, a touchstone by means of which postulated Bible-based environmental ethics may be assayed.

White's Conclusion From Genesis: The Genesis Teleology and Its Applications Are Inherently Anthropocentric

If White's claims are justified, then White is correct in indicting Christianity as bearing "a huge burden of guilt" for environmental destruction (1206). Not only is Judeo-Christianity culpable presumably for the Genesis account *and* the application of it by its adherents, but also White alleges there to be responsibility beyond influencing those simply within Judeo-Christian traditions. He suggests that Christian attitudes regarding humanity and nature "are almost universally held not only by Christians and neo-Christians but also by those who fondly regard themselves as post-Christian" (ibid.). He regards it as inconsequential "that most people do not think of these attitudes as Christian," because "no new set of basic values has been accepted in our society to displace those of Christianity" (1207). Thus, White perceives certain problematic Christian ideas as permeating (at least) the Western world, and as primary causal factors of the present ecological crisis.

After diagnosing the offending tenets in general terms, White identifies the practical significance of Christian influence: "What we do about ecology depends on our ideas of the man-nature relationship" (1206). For White, the implications of Christianity (in both its theory and practice) are so negative and pervasive, that he sees no solution to the ecological crisis "until we find a new religion or rethink our old one" (ibid). In the closing statements of his essay, White restates the problem in two different ways. First, he laments that "we shall continue to have a worsening ecological crisis until we reject the Christian axiom that nature has no reason for existence save to serve man" (1207). Next, he warns that our present efforts in science and technology "are so tinctured with orthodox

Christian arrogance toward nature that no solution for our ecological crisis can be expected from them alone" (ibid.).

White's prescription, that the Christian axiom of human functional superiority over nature must be rejected, represents his understanding (in summary) of Genesis teleology. White reasons that because man shares God's transcendence of nature and has a monopoly on spirit, he is thus the intended master of nature. As a result, White perceives that all nonhuman nature without any exception, in fact, was planned and purposed to serve that end; and that it is God's revealed will that humanity exploit nature to that end. In short, White perceives that the creation story places humanity (and perhaps, man, more specifically) at the center of all created things. Thus, while each of White's seven particular claims invites examination of the textual evidence, that examination must consider White's broader and more central allegation: *that the Genesis teleology is overtly anthropocentric.*

White's recognition regarding the inefficacy of current scientific and technological pursuits to resolve the environmental crisis represents his understanding (in summary) of the historically negative impact of Judeo-Christian undergirding as an application of Genesis teleology. White perceives that science and technology will be unable on their own to resolve challenges caused by anthropocentric teleology because those tools have historically been grounded in the very anthropocentrism they would be used to counter. White notes that Christianity made exploitative attitudes toward nature possible, and further considers that much of Western science is grounded in such exploitation. Because the old inhibitions to exploitation of nature were destroyed presumably by the triumph of the creation story and its adherents over paganism, the pursuits of science and technology were unencumbered by concerns for nature. Again, White points an accusing finger at the Genesis account and subsequent applications, because he perceives them as tainting Western human interaction with nonhuman nature. In particular, White concludes that it is the anthropocentrism of Genesis that has led to the misguided goals and methods of science and technology.

For White then, his cumulative case points to a Genesis worldview that is anthropocentric at its core. He interprets Genesis as presenting a vast dichotomy between humanity and nature, with humanity having intrinsic value through the *imago Dei*, and nature possessing only instrumental value insofar as it is designed to serve man's purposes. For White, it is this anthropocentric principle inherent in the creation story that dooms (at least Western interpretations of) Christianity to primary culpability for the ecological crisis and to irrelevance in trying to resolve it. While White's handling of relevant evidence and testimony is at times suspect, his general conclusion that anthropocentrism is a primary evil is not so questionable. What bears further examination is whether or not anthropocentrism is rooted in Genesis, as White suggests.

6

Considering Anthropocentrism: Definitions and Models

White's anthropocentric indictment of Christianity is communicated plainly. Elsewhere, he reinforces the theme, saying, "The world had been created by God for the spiritual edification of man, and served no other purpose."[1] He adds that the anthropocentrism of late antiquity and the early Middle Ages was "extreme."[2] For White the anthropocentrism of Genesis and its applications is unmistakable. In anticipation of investigating the Genesis text to determine the plausibility of White's claim, we must first understand the term anthropocentrism—not only as White applies it, but also as considered by more recent scholarship. Definition can help answer questions regarding the kind and degree of anthropocentrism we might expect to find in the Genesis account to support or counter White's claim.

It must be emphasized here as a matter of introduction, that the following discussion of value theory is not intended to be a comprehensive treatment of these ideas, for such a handling is well beyond the scope of this project. Instead these introductory ideas are included with a view to (1) clarifying the scope of White's allegation of anthropocentrism against the Judeo-Christian tradition—and Genesis in particular, and

1. White, "Natural Science," 424.

2. Ibid.

in anticipation of examining the evidence of Genesis, (2) setting forth a basic framework whereby the value claims of Genesis can be evaluated.

At first glance the distinction between anthropocentrism and nonanthropocentrism seems fairly straightforward; but environmental philosophers have highlighted the complexity of the dichotomy. Callicott suggests that anthropocentric axiology "confers intrinsic value on human beings and regards all other things, including other forms of life, as being only instrumentally valuable, i.e., valuable only to the extent that they are means or instruments which may serve human beings."[3] Though varied in certain nuances, anthropocentrism refers to basic human-centeredness and human-only intrinsic value. Nonanthropocentrism also can be understood to take a variety of forms. Callicott further observes that a nonanthropocentric axiology "would confer intrinsic value on some non-human beings."[4] Zoocentrism and biocentrism, for example, are nonanthropocentric models that center on and recognize intrinsic value of animals and life, respectively, rather than specifically focusing on and limiting intrinsic value to human life.

Neither zoocentrism nor biocentrism, however, is particularly compatible with a redacted dominionism reading of Genesis. Finnish environmental philosopher Leena Vilkka describes zoocentrism as "a philosophy in which the issues, concepts and values of animals are central,"[5] underscoring a naturalistic cosmology at odds with the theistic cosmology perceived by the EC as pervasive in the Genesis account. Paul Taylor, a leading proponent of biocentrism, highlights a key tenet of what might be called "strong biocentrism"—species impartiality, affirming "one who accepts that doctrine regards all living things as possessing inherent worth—the *same* inherent worth, because no species has been shown to be 'higher' or 'lower' than any other."[6] Weaker versions of biocentrism have been suggested by, for example, Kenneth Goodpaster and Holmes Rolston III, in which intrinsic value is distributed unequally among organisms depending on their unequal (or at least different) capacities.[7] Agreeing with Taylor in this particular, redacted dominionism will argue for the equal value of all created things, but not equal intrinsic

3. Callicott, "Non-Anthropocentric Value Theory," 299.

4. Ibid.

5. Vilkka, *Intrinsic Value of Nature*, 37.

6. P. Taylor, "Ethics of Respect," 181.

7. Goodpaster, "Being Morally Considerable" 308–25; and Rolston, *Considering Natural Value*, 167–202.

value. Rather, redacted dominionism will argue that all creatures from man to the birds of the air, the fishes of the sea, the beasts creeping on dry land are instrumentally valuable to God in equal measures, each in its own way. Redacted dominionism assumes different cosmological premises from Taylor's essentially evolutionary cosmology and ascribes the same moral function to all—to be fruitful to multiply their various species populations. Biocentrists, whether strong or weak, take most if not all organisms other than humans to be moral patients but not to be moral agents, beings that can have moral obligations or responsibilities toward others. In sharp contrast to biocentrism, redacted dominionism assigns to all God's creatures both equal instrumental value to God and equal doxological obligations to God.

Of particular use to the project at hand is theocentrism—a nonanthropocentric model compatible with an evangelical reading of the early Genesis narrative and one that allows for the essentially equitable value of all created things within a theistic cosmology. Hope College professor of religion, Steven Bouma-Prediger, understands theocentrism to imply that "man is not the measure of all things and the sole test of the worth of creation," and that "God, not humanity is at the center of things."[8] Bouma-Prediger's comment raises a question of value. If God is at the center, rather than humanity, then what kind of value does humanity possess? While theocentrists such as Bouma-Prediger and Calvin DeWitt argue for the intrinsic value of all creatures, redacted dominionism will assert that no created thing has intrinsic value, but instead, all creatures have instrumental value—to serve the purposes of God, and consequently all creatures have essentially equitable value, even if they differ in functionality.

It should be noted here that even as nonanthropocentrism has received its share of nuanced treatment, so likewise has anthropocentrism. Environmental philosopher Bryan Norton identifies a common assumption shared by anthropocentric and nonanthropocentric perspectives alike: that human beings are considered to be the source of all values.[9] To alleviate this perspectival problem (regardless of the viewpoint, humanity is still the primary valuator), Norton proposes a parsing of anthropocentrism into strong and weak forms—just as there may be strong and weak biocentrism. Of strong anthropocentrism, Norton

8. Bouma-Prediger, *Beauty of the Earth*, 103.

9. Norton, "Environmental Ethics," 164.

says, "A value theory is strongly anthropocentric if all value countenanced by it is explained with reference to satisfactions of felt preferences of human individuals."[10] He defines anthropocentrism as weak if "all value countenanced by it is explained by reference to satisfaction of some felt preference of a human individual or by reference to its bearing upon the ideals which exist as elements in a world view essential to determinations of considered preferences."[11] Strong anthropocentrism is "strongly consumptive,"[12] and consequently offers no grounds for judging exploitative behavior, because humanity sets value based on felt preferences and then proceeds to consume according to those preferences. Weak anthropocentrism provides for rational and irrational felt preferences, laying the groundwork to critique exploitative behavior, and emphasizes the closeness of human relations with nature. Consequently, in weak anthropocentrism Norton perceives "a framework for developing powerful reasons for protecting nature."[13]

Still, weak anthropocentrism does not seem to resolve entirely the problem of humanity determining the value of nature, or more directly, whether that value is ultimately objective or subjective. John O'Neill, environmental philosopher from Manchester University, describes the objectivist perspective of value as "that the evaluative properties of objects are real properties of objects, that they are properties that objects possess independently of the valuations of valuers, in contrast to the subjectivist consideration that "the source of all values lies in valuers."[14] Redacted dominionism decidedly favors a subjectivist theory of value, in one sense, and an objectivist theory in another. All people, animals, and plants (all life on earth) have value determined by the (presumably considered—it would be impious to think otherwise) preferences (however inscrutable they may be to us) of an Ultimate Valuer, God. In that sense its value theory is subjectivist. Because God, in the EC view, is independent of all human (and animal) subjectivity, God's valuing provides a universal—and thus, in that sense an objective—point of reference for determining value in the creation. Consequently, no value hierarchy exists among created things, from the point of view of

10. Ibid., 165.
11. Ibid.
12. Ibid.
13. Ibid.
14. O'Neill, "Varieties of Intrinsic Value," 135, 132.

redacted dominionism. All creatures are of equal instrumental value to God. Weak anthropocentrism does not altogether avoid White's critique of anthropocentrism, because only humans have intrinsic value and everything else has instrumental value—how much to be determined not by felt preferences but by considered human preferences. Whether or not White is right to think that any degree or kind of human superiority ultimately plays a negative role in human relations with nonhuman beings, redacted dominionism avoids both kinds of value hierarchy altogether. It avoids the intrinsic/instrumental value hierarchy and within each kind of value, it avoids the greater/lesser hierarchy. All creatures have equal instrumental value to God.

Returning to White's critique of anthropocentrism, in light of the above cursory review of value theory in environmental ethics, White attributes to Genesis, anthropocentric instrumental value theory. Humanity is at the center, because the *imago Dei* puts us there, assigning instrumental value to nature based on its utility for humans. Whether White attributes strong or weak anthropocentrism to Genesis is moot. He does say that it is God's will that man exploit nature for his *proper* ends. Charitably interpreted, "proper ends" could be read as "considered preferences." However, the overall tone and thrust of White's critique of alleged biblical anthropocentrism suggests that he has in mind what Norton later dubs strong anthropocentrism, God authorizing humans to maximize their felt preferences, by means of the ruthless exploitation of nature. It is this exploitative attitude toward nature that White strongly condemns, and it is this attitude that White warns must be stricken from our foundational (axiomatic) beliefs if the ecological crisis is to be effectively managed and reversed. And the only way it can be stricken from our axioms, White thinks, is by striking the creation narrative from the Bible. That, of course, the EC will not do. Consequently, in order for an evangelical environmental ethic to adequately answer White, it must ultimately counter the idea that the early Genesis narrative (and thus, the whole of Christian teleology) reflects an attitude of strong anthropocentrism. Addressing this issue is a point of focus in the chapters that follow, although there is no distinction drawn in them between strong and weak anthropocentrism, because redacted dominionism eschews anthropocentrism altogether in any form whatsoever.

7

Considering Genesis 1–2

THE GERMANE BIBLICAL DATA regarding value claims pertaining to the relationship of humanity to nonhuman beings is most plainly conveyed within the first nine chapters of Genesis. The Genesis 1–2 creation narratives (with Genesis 1 understood by the EC as presenting the divine viewpoint, and Genesis 2 offering the human perspective) provide particular insight into original teleology and man/nature relationships. More specifically 1:26–28 considers foundational aspects of these relationships, including ontological and functional value of humanity and nonhuman nature.

A comparison of the two narratives will consider whether or not they are consistent in their value claims. It is worth noting in this context that Callicott discusses White critically, observing that White set a low standard of biblical scholarship in that he readily conflates "the two very different geneses, Genesis-P and Genesis-J."[1] The question Callicott anticipates cannot be avoided: does Genesis represent two inconsistent sets of value claims? If so, could White's claims be both justified and countered alternately by the Genesis 1–2 narratives? These questions underscore the importance of comparing the two narratives insofar as they make value claims regarding man and nature.

As will be discussed in the next chapter, Genesis 3 introduces a dramatic shift with the episode of original sin and the fall of humanity, and consequently of all creation. Whether or not the events recounted here

1. Callicott, "Genesis Revisited," 71.

represent a significant reordering and alteration of human and nonhuman valuation is considered in light of the post-Fall value claims and mandates of 8:15—9:6, and in view of the pivotal verbiage of 9:7. As White says, "we cannot understand the fevers of our age until we arrive at the true historical diagnosis of the malady afflicting contemporary religion."[2] His comments are pertinent both to the Genesis situation—with its recounting of a universe-altering malady, as well as to present circumstances, wherein he seeks to diagnose the true cause of the current disease, suspecting Genesis to be the cause.

The passages considered in the following discussions are handled exegetically with primary dependence on the Hebrew Masoretic Text[3] with aid from the Greek Septuagint (LXX)[4] and from modern day English translations.[5] The Masoretic Text provides access to the earliest and most complete extant textual evidence in the original Hebrew language. The Greek LXX offers secondary support as an early translation. The English is utilized for interpretive accessibility to the reader. The interpretive approach employed is the literal grammatical-historical approach of the EC, though non-EC interpreters are occasionally considered—either for their reliance on similar hermeneutic methodology, or for relevant clarifications they might otherwise offer to the EC understanding.

Earlier, I suggested that if we are to discover an interpretation that can be viewed as valid in the EC for the purposes of grounding both a comprehensive and an equitable environmental ethic for all creatures, it seems the interpretation must meet at least the following criteria: (1) it must be justifiable from the text itself; (2) it ought to maintain the highest degree of textual integrity in applying EC methodology; (3) ideally, it should represent human and nonhuman beings as having equal value; and (4) consequently it would represent the strongest possible biblical environmental ethic, at least in answering White's anthropocentric

2. White, "Christian Myth," 145.

3. I utilize here an unpointed text (no vowels or tropes) with reliance on *Biblia Hebraica Stuttgartensia*: *With Westminster Hebrew Morphology*.

4. With primary reliance on *Septuaginta: With Morphology* and secondary reliance on Rahlfs, *Septuaginta*.

5. The primary English translation is the New American Standard Bible (NASB), because it attempts the highest degree of word for word representation and literalness in its translation. At times the translation can be wordy and even clumsy, and in such instances I may refer to the English Standard Version (ESV), which sometimes utilizes more contemporary phrasing.

indictment, because it is not grounded in anthropocentric theology, and avoids altogether a value hierarchy within the creation.

The exegetical analyses that follow in chapters 3 and 4 evaluate the early Genesis narrative and complementary passages, primarily to assess whether the four views (dominionism, stewardship, citizenship, and redacted dominionism) are justifiable from the biblical text within EC hermeneutic methodology, and secondarily, to consider the resulting value claims regarding human and nonhuman beings. If EC methodology results only in an anthropocentric perspective of the texts in question, then White's charges (for example) stand, and the EC would probably have to rely only on weak anthropocentrisms for response. Thus in consideration of biblical value claims, these chapters will also engage White's critiques as the biblical narrative warrants, as a complementary (to the four principles outlined above) means of testing the practical worth of the four interpretive models.

The argument made in these following chapters is that, applying EC methodology, redacted dominionism is the best interpretation of the biblical data, as it is able to reconcile the two creation narratives of Genesis 1 and 2, and to recognize the cosmological shift of Genesis 3 as rendering Genesis 1:26ff a snapshot of what once was and might have remained but for the events of the Fall. Further, redacted dominionism is able to reconcile these three contexts with the value claims of Genesis 9. Consequently, redacted dominionism provides a coherent grounding of a viable biblical environmental ethic that can counter, for example, White's critiques.

GENESIS 1:26—THE DOMINION MANDATE AND THE IMAGO DEI

וַיֹּאמֶר אֱלֹהִים נַעֲשֶׂה אָדָם בְּצַלְמֵנוּ כִּדְמוּתֵנוּ וְיִרְדּוּ בִדְגַת הַיָּם וּבְעוֹף
הַשָּׁמַיִם וּבַבְּהֵמָה וּבְכָל־הָאָרֶץ וּבְכָל־הָרֶמֶשׂ הָרֹמֵשׂ עַל־הָאָרֶץ

καὶ εἶπεν ὁ θεός Ποιήσωμεν ἄνθρωπον κατ᾽ εἰκόνα ἡμετέραν καὶ καθ᾽ ὁμοίωσιν, καὶ ἀρχέτωσαν τῶν ἰχθύων τῆς θαλάσσης καὶ τῶν πετεινῶν τοῦ οὐρανοῦ καὶ τῶν κτηνῶν καὶ πάσης τῆς γῆς καὶ πάντων τῶν ἑρπετῶν τῶν ἑρπόντων ἐπὶ τῆς γῆς.

Then God said, "Let Us make man in Our image, according to Our likeness; and let them rule over the fish of the sea and over

> the birds of the sky and over the cattle and over all the earth, and over every creeping thing that creeps on the earth."

To understand the way the Genesis narratives portray humanity, we must first understand the way humanity relates to God, a relationship revealed in the Genesis 1:26 discussion of the creation of humanity in God's image. This verse introduces us to the ontological nature of mankind and to the responsibility that follows. The passage begins with ויאמר (*wayo 'mer*,[6] vav consecutive[7] with Qal imperfect verb, third person singular), corresponding to καὶ εἶπεν (*kai eipen*, third person singular aorist active indicative verb), "And he said." [8]אלהים (*ĕlohim*, noun, masculine, plural) is often (though not exclusively) used to connote the proper Deity of the Hebrew Bible. The singular verb in this case indicates that common connotation pertains here, as is evidenced by the LXX rendering of the word as ὁ θεός (*ho theos*), with the definite article and the singular noun.

It is a common assertion by Christian commentators that the Hebrew plural noun, when used of the Deity, anticipates the later developing trinitarian idea of God.[9] Augustine suggests, for example, that the distinction between persons in the trinitarian deity is first observed in Genesis 1:2,[10] drawing a distinction (and yet a connection) between God and the spirit of God. The distinction is further considered from the perspective of the second person of the Trinity (cf. Isa 48:12 and 16) who characterizes himself as creator (48:13). In contrast, Judaic commentators do not perceive the employment of the Hebrew plural in identifying God as significant, recognizing it as a simple proper reference to a monotheistic God.[11]

6. Transliteration of the Hebrew follows the *Biblia Hebraica Stuttgartensia: With Westminster Hebrew Morphology*. Hebrew and Greek terms are transliterated here in their first appearances to aid the reader.

7. A vav prefixed to imperfect verbs in certain sequence (particularly following a perfect verb) usually causes the imperfect verb to be understood as a perfect, thus expressing the narrated past. The vav consecutive is also sometimes referred to as a vav conversive. See Kelley, *Biblical Hebrew*, 145; and Kittel et al, *Biblical Hebrew*, 7.

8. Notably, the singular *eloah* is elsewhere sometimes used, but the dual form, *elohiayim*, is not, and most commonly the plural *elohim*—which generally implies three or more—is used.

9. For example Augustine, *City of God*, bk. 7, ch. 11; and Sacks, *Lion and the Ass*, 45.

10. Augustine, *City of God*, bk. 7, ch. 11.

11. Rashi, for example makes no comment on the use of the plural, other than to acknowledge simple reference to God. See Ben Isaiah and Sharfman, *Pentateuch and*

In the context of discerning the ontological value of man, the implications of this plural language about God are significant.[12] Shlomo Yitzhaki (Rashi), an eleventh-century French Rabbi noted for his literalistic hermeneutic,[13] and Philo, a first-century Alexandrian philosopher noted for his nonliteral hermeneutic,[14] for example, both suggest that the plural pronouns in Genesis 1:26 (in our image and after our likeness) reference God *and* the angels (Philo asserts that the angels were assistants who could later be blamed for humanity's contrary actions) rather than God alone, while Keil and Delitzsch, collaborating nineteenth-century German exegetes, strongly disagree.[15] Swiss Reformer Karl Barth also disagrees that the Latin *pluralis majestatis* (plural of majesty) is in view here, suggesting that it is "quite foreign to the linguistic usage of the Old Testament."[16]

The verb phrase itself is also significant. Whereas Genesis 1 recounts six days of creation, after Genesis 1:3 each creative act is prefaced by ויאמר אלהים—"and God said," and in each case, the verb is singular while the noun is plural. This instance of the phrase in 1:26 is the last occurrence preceding a creative event, but it also represents the first time the creative event is preceded by deliberation on God's part. This seems a point of perspectival interest, drawing the reader's attention to an aspect of distinctiveness of the soon-to-be-created human race. Further, earlier creative acts were described in brief as accomplished by the speaking, whereas the discussion of man takes a different tone. There is deliberation, and distinctive methodology is employed in the creation of man. For some, this narrative shift might represent the beginning of the anthropocentric idea, because the text records in more detail the planning and actual creation of man than any other created thing discussed in either of the two creation narratives.

Rashi's Commentary, 1, 14.

12. For example see Chazan, "Barcelona 'Disputation,'" 824–42.

13. Ben Isaiah and Sharfman, *Pentateuch and Rashi's Commentary*, 14.

14. Philo, *Works of Philo*, 11.

15. "The plural 'We' was regarded by the fathers and earlier theologians almost unanimously as indicative of the Trinity: modern commentators . . . as pluralis majestatis . . . or as communicative, an address to the spirits or angels who stand around the Deity and constitute His council . . . either . . . the spirits took part in the creation of man; or it reduces the plural to an empty phrase . . . Moreover, this . . . is irreconcilable with the words 'in our image, after our likeness; since man was created in the image of God alone . . .'" Keil and Delitzsch, *Commentary on the Old Testament*, 1:38.

16. Barth, *Church Dogmatics*, 191.

The verb נעשה (*na ʿăšeh*, Qal imperfect first person plural cohortative verb) is rendered in the LXX as Ποιήσωμεν (*poiesomen*, first person plural aorist active subjunctive verb) is translated as "Let us make." The repeated disagreement in number between the verbs and nouns shows a deliberate distinction between persons and invites the reader to consider whether or not angels are included in this discussion or whether an internally or personally trinitarian deity is in view. Further, in this case the doing or making here is not creation out of nothing, from the Latin *ex nihilo* (as 2:7 identifies the ingredients used) and the aorist of the LXX implies a punctiliar event rather than a process.

If this is properly understood as punctiliar, then there is tension between the Genesis creation account and the idea of macroevolution. C.A. Briggs, nineteenth-century professor at Union Theological Seminary, provides an early attempt at resolving this conflict through genre characterization. He suggests that while "the first chapter of the Bible gives a representation of the creation of the world," it should not be interpreted literally as historical account.[17] Further, Briggs asserts that the text shows eight characteristics of poetic literature.[18] The genre explanation is unsuitable to more literalistic interpreters like evangelical theologian Henry Morris, who considers the Gospel records of Jesus's acceptance of Genesis as "literal history" to be evidence that the Genesis account is historical narrative rather than poetic literature.[19] Such are the hermeneutic challenges in approaching Genesis.

17. Briggs, "Hebrew Poem," 273. "It has generally been held that the author designs to give us the doctrine of the creation of the universe in a simple prose narrative, stating the creations as they occurred day after day in their orderly succession, until the whole universe was completed with all its contents in six days . . . But the author of the first chapter of Genesis does not propose to gives us a history of the creation of the universe out of nothing . . . He does not give us a prose history or a prose treatise of creation, but he presents us with a poem of the creation, a graphic and popular delineation of the genesis of the most excellent organism of our earth and heaven with their contents; . . . Our Poem of the Creation rises above the strifes of theologians and men of science and appeals to the esthetic taste and imagination of the people of God in all lands and in all times" (274).

18. "(1) similar parallelism between Assyrian and Akkadian poetry, (2) regular measurement of lines and words, (3) considerable number of archaic words found elsewhere only in poetry, (4) strophical organization (e.g., "and there was evening and morning"), (5) certain catch words of Hebrew poetry (e.g., "and God said," "and it was so," "and God saw that it was good"), (6) poetic license in archaic endings, (7) language and style as typical of poetry and unusual for prose, and (8) harmony and simplicity of thought." Briggs, "Hebrew Poem," 274–76.

19. Morris, *Genesis Record*, 31ff.

Robert Sacks, professor at St. Johns College, recognizes the danger in making a genre commitment before conducting an analysis of the text.[20] Sacks's analytical approach concludes in favor of a deliberately and intricately crafted historical narrative and not poetic lore. Whether or not the text is positing God's method of creation (as a literal interpretation would suggest) or simply communicating man's divine origin (as a figurative interpretation would conclude) is not the definitive point in determining value of man and nature (both methods recognize man's divine origin). While this nuanced distinction between the results of a literal versus figurative method in this instance is significant for other philosophical and theological reasons, its more detailed handling is beyond the scope of this present project, and will be left to others. Still, the issue underscores the need for caution and consideration when approaching the text of Genesis.

The object to be created is אדם, (*adam*, noun, masculine, singular, absolute), from a word meaning red, references the dirt from which the first man was made (cf. with Gen 2:7, מן האדמה (*min-ha 'ădamah*, from the dust) and shows an important nexus between the perspectives of the two Genesis creation accounts (with chapter 1 using the term to reference mankind collectively, and chapter 2 using the term to reference specifically the first man). In contrast, the LXX translates אדם as ἄνθρωπον (*anthropon*), a generic term that shows no direct relation to the dirt of 2:7 (lit., dust, χοῦν, choun). In the LXX some degree of connection between the two accounts is lost in translation.

The Hebrew idea that אדם is made מן הֲדמָה provides what can be understood within EC framework as a nonanthropocentric point of humility in that man is not fashioned of the same stuff comprising deity, but he is instead at the core rather base and ordinary. In this aspect man appears as part of nature and does not seem to transcend it. The following phrases, however, add definition and significance to the inaugural human condition. Man's essence is not merely dust, but rather is marked by two unique qualities not attributed to any other aspect of creation: (1) בצלמנו (bəṣ*aləmēnû,* preposition with masculine singular noun and first person plural suffix)—in our image, and (2) כדמותנו (*kidəmûtēnû,* preposition

20. Sacks recognizes that, "it has become the custom to preface and work of this nature with a discourse concerning Methods of Interpretation, and yet it is difficult to see how that can be done. To do so would presuppose that we already know how to read the book before we begin . . . we risk the danger of reading the book by a method foreign to the intent of the author." Sacks, *Lion and the Ass*, 30.

with masculine singular noun and first person plural suffix)—after our likeness.

Though the exact nature of the *imago Dei* is perhaps indeterminable from the text of Genesis, the practical implication of these characteristics is apparent immediately in 1:26, as the vav consecutive precedes the verb, וירדו (*wəyirədû*, Qal imperfect verb, third person masculine), which may be translated as let them rule or have dominion. The function of ruling is directly related (as the vav consecutive indicates) to the qualities of being in the image and likeness of God, and it is apparent that the image and likeness provide the necessary conditions for the ruling.

Notably, then the function of ruling is connected to the image and likeness, and the reader can anticipate that if a change in status occurs regarding the image and the likeness, then a reciprocal change in the function might also be expected. Nonetheless, at this juncture the intended function is ruling. Regarding the character of the rule or dominion four interpretations are considered: (1) dominionism, represented by Lynn White's despotic reading; (2) redefined dominionism, represented by stewardship or managerial anthropocentrism; (3) the citizenship view proposed by Callicott; and (4) redacted dominionism.

White's assertion that nature exists to serve man's purposes is undergirded by his premise that man shares God's transcendence over nature. And though he certainly perceives this point to be the epicenter of the inadequacy of the Judeo-Christian understanding of cosmology, he is not alone in his interpretation that Genesis 1:26 promotes human dominion over nature. Theodore Hiebert, professor at McCormack Theological Seminary, for example, describes this initial creation account as placing humanity in a unique priestly role, and one that represents extensive authority over nature.[21] He recognizes that this particular reading identifies an inaugural condition that remains unchanged by later events, and thus ruling and dominion are at the very core of the human vocation. Ian McHarg is representative of a host of interpreters who see

21. "Viewed from this priestly perspective, the human vocation of Genesis 1 is one of impressive authority and control. It is based on a hierarchical view of nature and society in which the human being, like the priest, was assigned special status and power. It is a view of the human vocation—and this must be kept in mind in discussions of the legacy of this concept—reflecting the self-understanding and particular social location of the ancient Israelite priesthood." Hiebert, "Human Vocation," 138.

the dominionist conclusion as a natural result of interpreting the Genesis account literally.[22]

Jamieson, Fausset, and Brown, collaborative nineteenth-century evangelical commentators, draw several important conclusions regarding dominionism from Genesis 1:26. They acknowledge that humanity has a delegated supremacy, which is rooted in the image of God as possessed by man. Additionally they cite Psalm 8:6–8 to indicate that the qualification (and thus the authority) remains unchanged, presupposing that Psalm 8 speaks of mankind as a whole and describes man's present and ongoing condition.[23] Matthew Poole, seventeenth-century English theologian, describes the conditions (i.e., nature) into which man arrived as being suitably prepared by God for "man's use and comfort."[24]

These interpreters suggest, then, that the evidence of Genesis shows that man presently has dominion over nature because man is uniquely connected to God in a relationship that remains unaltered. Dominionism interprets the *subdue* and *rule* imperatives of 1:28 naturally, or literally, yet with no consideration of later development, restriction, or recanting of these imperatives. Thus in this tradition, man is to govern nature. Sacks identifies this as the accurate understanding of the text, asserting that the terms imply that not only was man the pinnacle of creation, but he was that for which it was all made.[25]

There are two basic streams of dominionism (from a despotic reading): (1) moderate, and (2) consistent (in that it consistently applies the despotic reading, taking the implications to the fullest extent). The moderate form recognizes the dominion imperative and applies the ethical implications (primarily, that man is to fulfill his mandate through the domination and subjugation of the rest of creation), but not to their fullest degree. For example, in this form the imperative provides the impetus for scientific pursuit—much like Newton's thinking God's thoughts after him. This approach does not, however, recognize the eschatological implications that follow (namely, perpetual progress leading to the triumph

22. "Apparently, the literal interpretation of the creation in Genesis is that tacit text for Jews and Christians alike—man exclusively divine, man given dominion over all life and nonlife, enjoined to subdue the earth. The cosmos is thought to be a pyramid erected to support man upon its pinnacle; reality exists only because man can perceive it; indeed, God is made in the image of man." McHarg, "Place of Nature," 1–12.

23. Jamieson et al, *Commentary*, 8.

24. Poole, *Commentary on the Holy Bible*, 4.

25. Sacks, *Lion and the Ass*, 46.

of man over nature—including victory over his own nature). The more consistent domionism acknowledges the dominion mandate with a view to the mandate for scientific pursuit, and also recognizes and pursues actively the eschatological ramifications whether through postmillennialism or amillennialism—two traditions that have had significant influence in world affairs over at least the past millennium.[26]

More recently, and perhaps in response to later developing criticisms of the dominionism view, a stewardship or managerial anthropocentric interpretation has come into prominence. This second major interpretive tradition is a redefined dominionism. Simply put, this interpretation softens the *subdue* and *rule* imperatives by redefining the terms. Norbert Lohfink, professor of OT at Sankt Georgen Seminary, for example, suggests the meaning of וירדו is better rendered as shepherd rather than rule.[27]

Ruling, in this stewardship interpretation, references more stewardship than domination. Henry Morris's comments show the subtle distinction between dominionist and stewardship interpretations. He first describes that humanity has a dual commission, first to conquer and rule, then to pursue science and technology. These observations might be consistent with dominionism, however Morris shows a subtle departure from the dominionist interpretation in his observation that the dominion mandate "established man as God's steward over the created world and all things herein . . . The problem is, of course, that man has failed in his stewardship. Instead of using the earth for good, under God, he has denied God and abused his stewardship."[28] Morris's view is notably less anthropocentric than dominionism, because it considers man in a more subservient role (instead of humanity sharing God's position at the top, mankind is an intermediary), yet it still represents nature as a uniquely prepared habitation for humanity.

Shalom Rosenberg, of The Hebrew University of Jerusalem, and one who shares the stewardship view and uses similar hermeneutic methodology to the EC in deriving it, moves a bit further from anthropocentrism, as he notes that the *Torah*—in the totality of the

26. Postmillennialism references the second coming of the Messiah after a millennium (from Rev 20:1–6), or golden age of a globally victorious church. Amillennialism is the view that there is no literal millennial reign of a returned Messiah, but instead he reigns only spiritually at present through the church. Thus in similar fashion to postmillennialism the church is prophetically understood to be globally victorious.

27. As cited by Rogerson, *Genesis 1–11*, 19.

28. Morris, *Genesis Record*, 77.

commandments—represents "a distinctive Jewish ecological ethos . . . an ethos of respect for nature and for God's creation."[29] Further, Rosenberg deduces that "man is placed in the Garden not as an autocratic ruler, but as one who must preserve it, protect it, worry about it, and as one (like Noah in the subsequent generation) who must save the animals who are faced with the danger of extinction."[30] The basic tenets of the stewardship interpretation include an acknowledgement that humanity is separate from nature, and that humanity has been commissioned, in light of the transcendence man possesses, to care properly for the resources with which man interacts. Importantly, both Morris and Rosenberg recognize that later events (Morris cites sin, while Rosenberg notes Noahic stewardship) affect human responsibility.

In considering the viability of stewardship, Sacks recognizes two important characteristics of the ruling (1:26) and the dominion (1:28). He notes that the latter word is the same as that used to describe the relationship between the sun and the day (1:16), and he understands that the initial condition and resulting imperative is altered by later events—the consideration of which is necessary for the proper estimation of man's role in and relation to nature.[31] Rashi anticipates the possibility of such alteration when he observes that if man "is not found worthy he becomes subservient before them and the beast rules over him."[32] Beeson Divinity School's OT professor, Allen Ross states plainly that dominion was the initial intent, but citing Hebrews 2:8, sin adjusted the trajectory.[33] Rashi, Ross, Sacks, Morris, Rosenberg et al anticipate the significance of the Genesis 3 events and their affect on man's relationship to nature. But in a pre-Genesis 3 world, whether by dominion or stewardship, man's superiority over and separateness from nature seems apparent, as deduced from a literal understanding of Genesis 1:26.

While dominionism and stewardship share some common elements, they also contrast in certain aspects. In light of the documentary hypothesis,[34] Callicott reluctantly acknowledges textual grounding for both views, citing "two different and even contradictory messages re-

29. Rosenberg, "Concepts of Torah and Nature," 219.

30. Ibid., 220.

31. Sacks, *Lion and the Ass*, 46.

32. Ben Isaiah and Sharfman, *Pentateuch and Rashi's Commentary*, 14.

33. Ross, "Genesis," 29.

34. The theory of multiple authorship of the Torah.

specting the appropriate place and role of people in relation to the rest of creation."[35] Callicott recognizes that Genesis 1 puts forth a dominionist model, but that the first creation narrative (Gen 1–2:4) is a "Hellenized upstart" borrowing from Greek cosmology, and should be put aside as unworthy of consideration.[36]

Further, he understands Genesis 2:4—4:26 to be the older, more worthy text of the two, and that it describes Adam's design as "to be custodian or steward of creation."[37] He acknowledges the two resulting Judeo-Christian interpretive traditions: (1) the despotic interpretation, in which God's intent is that man be master and nature slave, and in which man is to subdue creation, and which represents a "weak, indirect, anthropocentric environmental ethic"; and (2) the stewardship interpretation, the case for which Callicott suggests is built seen through the lens of the Genesis 2 creation account and resulting in a "responsible but utilitarian, benign but authoritarian vice-regency of man over nature."[38]

Perhaps sensing key deficiencies in both dominionism and stewardship, Callicott recognizes that the events of Genesis 3 represent a cataclysmic change in fundamental aspects of the human condition and vocation, which events he accounts for by introducing a third interpretation he labels the citizenship interpretation.[39] In this view, mankind does not have any metaphysical distinction from nature, and was created to live harmoniously with nature. The citizenship view includes an interesting hamartialogy, in that "anthropocentrism itself is man's original sin and is responsible for the famous Fall."[40]

Though Callicott does not recognize the legitimacy of the dominion mandate as authentic to the Genesis record, his citizenship approach nonetheless underscores a problem that neither dominionism nor stewardship addresses: if they ever existed at all (of course, the EC suggests they did), the conditions proposed in Genesis 1:26 did not extend beyond the events of Genesis 3, and it would be careless to assume without warrant that a function (ruling) essentially dependent on a condition (the image and likeness of God) would continue unencumbered despite

35. Callicott, *Defense of the Land Ethic*, 138.

36. Callicott, *Beyond the Land Ethic*, 203.

37. Callicott, *Defense of the Land Ethic*, 138.

38. Callicott, *Earth's Insights*, 15–16, 17.

39. Ibid., 19.

40. Ibid.

alteration of the condition. In light of this shift, a fourth interpretation is considered here: that Genesis 1:26–28 then represents a snapshot, a moment in time, of an initial intention later adjusted, revised—in a word, redacted.

If the ruling of humanity is grounded in the qualities of being made in the image and likeness of God, it seems evident that the ruling or stewardship is to be conducted in accordance with that likeness and image. To understand, then, the character of the ruling, one would have to examine thoroughly how God rules his creation. Such an examination is beyond the scope of the task at hand; however, suffice it to say that we should understand that initially man's dominion was to reflect God's general outlook on nature, and that as man's condition changed his dominion was redacted.

This fourth interpretive approach is, therefore, redacted dominionism. It considers a textual argument from Genesis 9:7, in which God gives the multiplication and scattering imperatives but notably excludes the subduing and ruling imperatives. The theological argument here is that man indeed had dominion initially when perfectly equipped to administer it. But the fall of man created several problems that rendered man incapable of governing anything correctly, hence the initial dominion mandate was redacted. Also, the argument builds on the textual construction of 1:26, which makes use of the vav consecutive with the verb (וירדו) and thus connects the ruling with the condition of bearing the *imago Dei*.

If that image is tarnished or altered (as Rashi implies) then the imperative is noticeably affected. From the first genealogy (Gen 5) it is evident that the image has been altered by the Fall, as Adam sires a son not in God's image, but in his own. This would be consistent with the exclusion of the dominion imperative in 9:7. In addition to the tarnishing or alteration of God's image in man, man suffers the noetic effects of sin— newfound deficiencies of the mind. These are understood not only to limit him spiritually, but also in his interaction with the world around him. Additionally, Genesis 3:17–19 indicates that the ground would be increasingly difficult to work with, thus the ease with which mastery might have previously been considered is now gone. Finally, 9:3 indicates that the animals would become primarily difficult to manage, due to their newfound fear of mankind.

Returning to the text of Genesis 1:26, we are introduced to the scope of this ruling as relating to five particular groups. First is בדגת הים (*bidgat hayam,* feminine singular noun with preposition prefix, and noun with article) with the ב (*bet*) preposition rendered by most translations as over with the feminine singular noun fish (דגת) in construct relationship to the articulated masculine singular noun ים (*yam*) or sea. Rashi, for example, notes that the ideas of dominion and subservience are present in the preceding word (וירדו).[41] If these ideas are indeed present, then the translation of the preposition as over would be appropriate. Further, the LXX translates the ב preposition appearing before each of the five groups with the genitive plural article τῶν (*ton*). The Hebrew employs the singular in each case, while the LXX translates each as plural.

Second, is ובערף השמים (*ûbə ʿôp hašamayim*), a vav consecutive and preposition with masculine singular noun fowl or flying creature in construct relationship to the articulated masculine plural noun heavens. Third is ובבהמה (*ûbabhēmah*), a vav consecutive and preposition with masculine singular noun beast or creeping animal. The first three groups over which man was to rule—the fish of the sea, the bird of the heavens, and the beasts of the field—correspond to all three categories of living things created on day five (Gen 1:20–23), and up to that point on day six (1:24–25).

The fourth sphere of human rule is ובכל־הארץ (*ûbəkal-ha ʾareṣ*), a w (*vav*) consecutive, ב preposition, and כל (*kal*) conjunction with an articulated feminine singular noun, and over all the land or earth. Whereas the range of human rule in the first three aspects might be limited to the fish, the birds, and the beasts, and not the environment in which these were to live, this fourth locale is unlimited. The term הארץ (*ha ʾareṣ*) used here is also used in 1:1, to signify all (identified) created reality that was not השמים, *the heavens*. The LXX translates הארץ as τῆς γῆς (tes ges), the genitive singular of the common word for the *earth* or the *world* in totality. Human rule was to be as universal as was physically possible.

The phrase ובכל־הרמש (*ûbəkal-haremeš*) includes the vav consecutive, preposition, conjunction, and adjective (ובכל, *ûbəkal*), and over all, with the articulated masculine singular noun (הרמש, *haremeš*) and articulated masculine singular participle (הרמש, *haromēš*), referencing the creeping creeper, whose environs was על־הארץ (*al-ha ʾareṣ*) upon the land or earth. Thus human rule was to extend to the land (or earth) itself, every living thing in it, and the living things in the sea and the heavens.

41. Ben Isaiah and Sharfman, *Pentateuch and Rashi's Commentary*, 14.

Taken at face value and separated from later verses, Genesis 1:26 appears to set a trajectory supportive of White's claims (as it would appear *prima facie* that all of creation was intended to serve man's purposes). However, one of them—that man shares God's transcendence of nature, is challenged by the idea that humanity was built from dirt—from nature itself. Man is named after the dirt from which he is made (cf. 1:26 and 2:7). The text, as literally interpreted, makes a point to note that man is a part of nature, rather than transcendent over it. For man to share God's transcendence of nature, there must be something added to his nature that would impute such transcendence. While this passage shows human uniqueness, privilege, and responsibility through the *imago Dei*, the text has not asserted that the *imago Dei* ascribes to man the transcendence White asserts (sharing God's transcendence over nature).

According to Genesis 1:26, man is made in the *imago Dei*, but it is very difficult to ascertain exactly what are the essential components of the *imago Dei*, and attempts at explaining this image are unsurprisingly diverse. Phyllis Bird, of Garrett-Evangelical Theological Seminary, recognizes the challenges of approaching the issue either from a strictly exegetical methodology, in which case there is little textual information available, or from a strictly dogmatic or theological approach, in which case conclusions derived are often not justifiable from the text itself.[42] Though she offers an extensive bibliography of modern writing on the issue, she perceives that the problem remains unresolved.[43]

Orthodox Jewish scholar Alexander Altmann identifies among rabbinic sources what he calls "a certain reluctance to define the meaning of the phrase."[44] He traces Aramaic sources that textually separate the image from God, and thus render the phrase in 1:27 as "God created man in an image," instead of God created man in His image.[45]

42. Bird suggests that, "A legacy of the long and intense theological interest in the imago Dei has been an atomizing and reductionist approach to the passage, in which attention is focused on a single phrase or clause, severing it from its immediate context and from its context within the larger composition, a fixation and fragmentation which has affected exegetical as well as dogmatic discussion. A further legacy of this history of speculation has been the establishment of a tradition of theological inquiry and argument with a corresponding body of knowledge separate from, and largely independent of, exegetical scholarship on the same passage." Bird, "'Male and Female,'" 130.

43. See Bird, "'Male and Female,'" 129fn2.

44. Altmann, "Homo imago Dei," 235.

45. Ibid., 236–39.

Philo speaks with uncharacteristic brevity on the specifics of *imago Dei*, concluding simply (albeit after lengthy philosophical discussion) that it references "an accurate impression, having a clear and evident resemblance in form."[46] Rashi says man "was made with a stamp like a coin which is made by means of a die . . . ," indicating that בצלם is to be understood literally, but offering no indication of how the face of that coin might have appeared.[47] Rashi's metaphor seems an appropriately limited one in light of its somewhat veiled antecedent. Considering Christian perspectives of the divine likeness, Barth critiques early church exegetes for their imbalance and inconsistency in approaching definitions of the *imago Dei*, specifically regarding whether it was purely spiritual or included physical elements as well.[48] Barth concludes that man is not created as the image of God, but rather in connection to it.[49]

Louis Berkhof, Reformed theologian from Calvin Theological Seminary, summarizes well the historical disagreements, pointing out that Socinians and early Arminians believed the *imago Dei* to extend only to man's dominion over the lower creation.[50] Baptist theologian Augustus Strong offers a definition that draws our attention to the essential and initial abilities and qualifications of humanity.[51] While these specific delineations are not explicitly expressed in the text, and consequently remain open to question, the value in Strong's observation is in the reciprocal relationship he identifies between one's nature and one's ability. If Strong is correct, then these interdependent characteristics may play a pivotal role in understanding the man/nature dichotomy—specifically as human nature changes from its pristine state in Genesis 1–2 to a fallen condition in Genesis 3. For now, we will not assume specific content of the *imago Dei* except to say: (1) it is of foundational importance to the Genesis 1

46. Philo, *Works of Philo*, 11.

47. Ben Isaiah and Sharfman, *Pentateuch and Rashi's Commentary*, 14–15.

48. Barth, *Church Dogmatics*, 192–94.

49. Barth says specifically that, "Man is not created to be the image of God . . . he is created in correspondence with the image of God . . . the point of the text is that God willed to create man as a being corresponding to His own being—in such a way that He Himself . . . is the original and prototype, and man the copy and imitation." Barth, *Church Dogmatics*, 197.

50. Berkhof, *Systematic Theology*, 202–3.

51. Strong asserts that, "As created in the natural image of God, man had a moral nature; as created in the moral image of God, man had a holy character. The first gave him natural ability; the second gave him moral ability." Strong, *Systematic Theology*, 514.

creation narrative, as it is assigned to humanity no less than three times in 1:27; (2) it seems equally borne by both man and woman, as 1:27 asserts the equality of man and woman in possessing the *imago Dei*;[52] (3) it seems the most fundamental characteristic of inaugural human nature; and (4) it seems a necessary prerequisite to the blessing and commission that follows in 1:28.

As a direct result of this ontological distinction from the rest of nature, mankind, in its initial and perfect state, was to rule or have dominion over the earth and all other living things (cf. Gen 1:26 and 1:28). Importantly, the *imago Dei* is the only reason given in the Genesis narrative for the dominion mandate, thus if there is later adjustment to human identity and qualification pertaining to the *imago Dei* (as there appears to be in Genesis 3), then it would not be surprising that the dominion mandate might be adjusted. That the mandate was adjusted in such a manner is suggested in chapter 3 when Genesis 3 and 8:15—9:7 are discussed.

Genesis 1:27 offers two points of interest: (1) the actualization of God's intention to create humanity in his own image, and (2) the equality of men and women in bearing God's image. As the centrality of the *imago Dei* has been discussed at length in the context of 1:26, and as the matter pertaining to the ontological equality of both sexes is more relevant to discussions of androcentrism (such as White's passing assertion that Eve was an afterthought) than to the present discussion of environmental ethics, and in order to facilitate the flow of the argument, a further consideration of 1:27 is not included in this chapter. Nonetheless, 1:28 is not silent about the relationship of man and woman, and their relationship to the rest of creation.

GENESIS 1:28—THE DOMINION MANDATE REITERATED

וַיְבָ֣רֶךְ אֹתָם֮ אֱלֹהִים֒ וַיֹּ֨אמֶר לָהֶ֜ם אֱלֹהִ֗ים פְּר֥וּ וּרְב֛וּ וּמִלְא֥וּ אֶת־הָאָ֖רֶץ
וְכִבְשֻׁ֑הָ וּרְד֞וּ בִּדְגַ֤ת הַיָּם֙ וּבְע֣וֹף הַשָּׁמַ֔יִם וּבְכָל־חַיָּ֖ה הָֽרֹמֶ֥שֶׂת עַל־הָאָֽרֶץ׃

καὶ ηὐλόγησεν αὐτοὺς ὁ θεὸς λέγων Αὐξάνεσθε καὶ πληθύνεσθε καὶ πληρώσατε τὴν γῆν καὶ κατακυριεύσατε αὐτῆς καὶ ἄρχετε τῶν ἰχθύων τῆς θαλάσσης καὶ τῶν πετεινῶν τοῦ οὐρανοῦ καὶ

52. "God created man in His own image, in the image of God He created him; male and female He created them" (Gen 1:27).

> πάντων τῶν κτηνῶν καὶ πάσης τῆς γῆς καὶ πάντων τῶν ἑρπετῶν τῶν ἑρπόντων ἐπὶ τῆς γῆς.
>
> God blessed them; and God said to them, "Be fruitful and multiply, and fill the earth, and subdue it; and rule over the fish of the sea and over the birds of the sky and over every living thing that moves on the earth."

The male and female (זכר ונקבה) of 1:27, taken together, function as the joint antecedent of the third person plural אתם. The blessing was for both. That God pronounced it both male and female is reinforced by the employment of the prepositional phrase, להם, (*lahem*, *to them*). Included in the blessing is a series of five imperatives with plural suffixes, further indicating that male and female together received this blessing and imperatives: (1) פרו (*pərû*)—you bear fruit, or be fruitful (Αὐξάνεσθε); (2) ורבו (*ûrəbû*) and you become great (or many, πληθύνεσθε); (3) ומלאו את־הארץ (*ûmilə'û 'et-ha 'areṣ*) and you fill the land (or you fill the earth, πληρώσατε τὴν γῆν); (4) וכבשהו—(*wəkibəšuha*) and you subdue (conquer and control, or lord over, κατακυριεύσατε) it; and (5) ורדו—(*ûrədû*) and you rule (or dominate, ἄρχετε).

The first three imperatives pertain to the proliferation of the species and to its dissemination throughout the whole of the earth. The significance of filling the whole earth is later emphasized (Gen 11), as the early urbanization at the tower of Babel represented a violation of this command as it was reiterated in Genesis 9:7. While there is no indication in the text as to God's motivation for these first three commands, one might legitimately wonder if at least part of the intent was to keep the creation from being disproportionately burdened as mankind became more numerous, and if so, then at least basic ecological considerations would not be foreign to God's designs for even a perfect world. Here one might consider that the early Genesis narrative presents the first human attempt at urbanization as a moral failure, as God apparently intended—at least initially—a more balanced human use of creation. It is worth noting that these early restrictions on human conduct challenge the veracity of White's assertion that Christianity is the world's most anthropocentric religion.

The second set of commands in Genesis 1:28 seem *prima facie* to support the anthropocentric idea. In no uncertain terms, the man and woman are commanded to conquer, control, and even dominate. Despite efforts on the part of some interpreters to soften the terminology to mean a stewardly or pastoral role rather than a governing one, the terms used (וכבשה ורדו) are, at least in the lexical sense, straightforward in their meanings, and more precisely translated in a despotic sense. Notre Dame ethics scholar Georges Enderle suggests, for example, as a consequence of increasing awareness of ecological problems, that certain "theological perspectives" should be developed, with no explanation of how such perspectives are justified by Genesis 1:26–28.[53] Enderle appeals to the European Ecumenical Assembly document "Peace with Justice for the Whole Creation" (1989) in support of his stewardship understanding.[54] Enderle and others assert the real meaning to be stewardship and not despotism, yet one of the words used in describing mankind's initial role is lexically translated as dominate. It is evident that the stewardship interpretation gives rise to a tension between the lexical meaning of the terminology found in the text and the theological and ethical motivations of stewardship interpreters.

The first set of imperatives in Genesis 1:28 (commands 1–3) place restrictions on mankind, at least implying a nonanthropocentric model. The second set (commands 4–5) places man in a central role in governing creation as God's representatives—being made in His image and likeness, as was established in 1:26. The subjects of mankind's rulership include the living things in the sea, the sky, and the land—in other words, man's dominion was apparently intended to be virtually universal.

In discussion of Genesis 1:26–28, Callicott reminds the reader of three interpretive traditions in Judeo-Christian perspective (despotic [or dominionism], stewardship, and citizenship), but a fourth interpretation is needed as (and if) the components of the early Genesis narrative are considered in concert. Whereas 1:26–28 do include a clear dominion mandate—as the despotic reading might emphasize—further narrative in the book shows the despotic condition to be only temporary in application. Likewise, the stewardship interpretation from 2:4 does not adequately account for the definitive verbiage of 1:26–28, which is quite

53. Enderle, "Common Ethical Ground," 177.

54. Enderle quotes: "So, we have to reconsider the prevailing ethics of recent centuries, which, in contrast to the real meaning of the Word of God, allowed humanity to 'dominate' the creation for its own ends, when, on the contrary, humanity should act as steward in service—service both of God and of the creation itself . . . " (ibid.).

vivid in its reference to human dominion, rule, domination,[55] subduing, and bringing into bondage.[56]

Finally, the metaphysical identity of man and nature, as the citizenship interpretation proposes, seems inconsistent with the 1:26–28 account. That is not a concern for the single known exponent of the citizenship interpretation, J. Baird Callicott, who regards Genesis 1 as an inauthentic, Johnny-come lately, impertinent add-on to the original Hebrew account of creation, which begins at Genesis 2:4. However unacceptable to the EC for that reason, from an EC perspective, Callicott's citizenship interpretation does uniquely (in comparison to the dominionism and stewardship interpretations) consider changed conditions after the Fall, and comes closest to the EC understanding, as I determine it to be, of the cause and significance of the Fall itself. If an exegetically viable environmental ethic for the EC is to be inferred from the Genesis account, one must consider the two distinct emphases of Genesis 1 and 2, along with the impact of the Fall, and post-Fall conditions. While resonant with my understanding of the impact of the Fall, the citizenship interpretation is incompatible with EC methodology, because it rejects Genesis 1. Likewise, dominionism, stewardship, and citizenship fall short of resolving the dissonance between Genesis 1 and Genesis 2, with its account of the Fall.

COMPARING THE GENESIS 1 AND 2 CREATION ACCOUNTS—DOMINIONISM OR STEWARDSHIP

As Eugene Merrill observes, "The consensus of critical scholarship is that the first 11 chapters of Genesis are not to be construed as genuine history."[57] Though there are a number of arguments to this end, perhaps the most potent is the seeming disparity between the creation narratives of Genesis 1 and 2, and in particular the distinct names for God employed in these contexts. The more common name, אלהים, is used thirty-five times in Genesis 1:1—2:3, and only eleven times in the remainder of Genesis 2, and in those latter instances only in conjunction with יהוה (*yəhwah*), which form is not used at all in Genesis 1. Of secondary concern is the

55. Brown et al, *Enhanced Brown-Driver-Briggs Hebrew and English Lexicon*, 921. (Hereafter, this resource is cited simply as BDB).

56. BDB 461.

57. Merrill, "Genesis 1–11 as Literal History," 75.

reference in 2:4 to a *day* of creation, which seemingly includes events from the six days of Genesis 1. Critics perceive these distinctions so pronounced as to necessitate at least two different sources entirely.

First let me address the putative six-day/one-day discrepancy. In consideration of the use of יום in Genesis 1 and 2, an ordinal does not precede ביום (*bəyôm,* in the day) in 2:4, whereas in chapter 1, in every instance after 1:5, an ordinal precedes יום. When accompanied by an ordinal, the term is more likely to reference a particular 24-hour day (e.g., first day, with evening and morning, etc.), whereas without an ordinal it can represent even very elongated periods of time (e.g., the day of the Lord, which in some cases can reference more than a thousand years). The omission of the ordinal in 2:4, while not clarifying source issues, may thus be used to resolve the apparent contradiction regarding the timeframes of chapters 1–2. In short, while questions regarding provenance persist, the two narratives may be seen to be not so discontinuous as to make contradictory value claims regarding the creative act itself or regarding the man and nature dichotomy.

Merrill sees unity in literary structure and theological themes.[58] Likewise, A. C. Gaebelein, nineteenth-century German evangelical theologian, perceives the text to possess both unity and continuity, recognizing the differences between the two accounts as perspectival rather than essential.[59] If Gaebelein is to be followed in his assertion that the differences are merely matters of perspective, then the second narrative can be viewed as agreeing with the first—that mankind indeed is at least somewhat distinct from other aspects of nature, and man (male and female alike) stood initially as ruler over it.

In light of the possibility of perspectival differences, the stewardship interpretation seems inadequate in that it does not suitably account for the rule and dominion commands of 1:26–28—imperatives that are not altered or redacted in Genesis 2. The issue then that the stewardship interpretation must resolve is how the rule and subdue passage can be understood as synonymous with the role assigned by God to Adam in

58. Ibid., 86.

59. A. C. Gaebelein observes that "There is . . . no contradiction between these two chapters. The second chapter in Genesis is not another history of creation nor does it contradict the account in the first chapter. The historical account of creation as a whole is found in Genesis i–ii:3. The division of chapters in the authorized version is unfortunate. From chapter ii:4 to the close of the chapter we have not a historical account of creation, but a divine statement of the relationships of creation, that is, man's place in it as its head." Gaebelein, *Annotated Bible,* 9.

Genesis 2. Without employing a deliberately nonliteral hermeneutic approach, the basic sense of the terminology employed seems to indicate that human function, as illustrated in 2:15 ("Then the Lord God took the man and put him into the garden of Eden to cultivate it and keep it") was merely an application of human ontological superiority over nature. In other words, the text does not seem to represent this activity as the complete fulfillment of the dominion mandate, but instead the cultivation and keeping is simply the outworking of a separate mandate altogether.

The terms of 2:15 are indicative of a vocation compatible with the stewardship interpretation. To cultivate (לעבדה, *lə ʿabədah*) here connotes the idea of working on behalf of or even serving.[60] The Qal form of the verb is used here, indicating that the man was to work on behalf of or serve the garden—it was not to serve him. The man exercised no dominion in choosing his locale, nor was his purpose in the garden to dominate it. To keep (ולשמרה, *ûləšamərah*) can alternately be translated as *watch*, or *preserve*.[61] This latter term especially supports the stewardship idea. Still, it is apparent that the garden mandate is not the equivalent of the earlier dominion mandate. Perhaps it could be said that the man/nature dichotomy in its Edenic application was one of human stewardship of nonhuman nature, but the original dominion mandate anticipated a much broader scope than this narrow geographic application discussed in Genesis 2. The earlier mandate was global in its scope.[62]

It seems then that dominion and stewardship may have been synchronic and unrelated aspects of the inaugural human condition, though neither independently accounts adequately for the evidence of the two creation narratives. In other words, mankind was to have dominion, and was also to steward, but the stewarding was not a qualifier or modifier of dominion, but rather an unrelated function, deriving from a divine intent (2:15) unrelated to the dominion mandate (1:26–28). Consequently, the unity of the two chapters is not compromised, as they may be understood not to be communicating two contradictory things, but rather two different things. To illustrate, X=black and X=white are contradictory statements. Whereas, to say X= black and X=soft is not to be contradictory, but rather to speak of two separate qualities. The distinctions between Genesis 1 and 2 may be understood

60. BDB 712.

61. BDB 1036.

62. Man was to fill the earth (Gen 1:28).

(though they have not historically) within EC methodology to be akin to the latter rather than the former example.

In noting this distinction between the first two chapters of Genesis, White recounts in a later writing that the most common charge against him in response to his "The Historical Roots" was that he "had ignorantly misunderstood the nature of 'man's dominion' and that it is not an arbitrary rule but rather a stewardship of our fellow creatures for which mankind is responsible to God."[63] Whether or not White misunderstands dominion, he certainly recognizes at least the historical tension between the two views. White commendably (in this writer's opinion) seems to find dominionism reprehensible and stewardship insufficient for grounding environmental solutions.

It seems then that dominionism and stewardship, to this point in the Genesis narrative, both lack textual justification within EC methodology. Further, they are both subject to at least aspects of White's critique. The citizenship view, being constructed on a premise (Genesis 1—2:4 is inauthentic) incompatible with EC thought, is inherently incapable of resolving the issue within EC framework. Still, the citizenship view handles the text following 2:4 perhaps more consistently than do the other two views and contains elements important to redacted dominionism, which will become apparent as we approach Genesis 9.

GENESIS 2:7—MANKIND DOES NOT SHARE GOD'S TRANSCENDENCE OF NATURE

> וַיִּיצֶר֩ יְהֹוָ֨ה אֱלֹהִ֜ים אֶת־הָֽאָדָ֗ם עָפָר֙ מִן־הָ֣אֲדָמָ֔ה וַיִּפַּ֥ח בְּאַפָּ֖יו נִשְׁמַ֣ת חַיִּ֑ים
> וַֽיְהִ֥י הָֽאָדָ֖ם לְנֶ֥פֶשׁ חַיָּֽה׃
>
> *καὶ ἔπλασεν ὁ θεὸς τὸν ἄνθρωπον χοῦν ἀπὸ τῆς γῆς καὶ ἐνεφύσησεν εἰς τὸ πρόσωπον αὐτοῦ πνοὴν ζωῆς, καὶ ἐγένετο ὁ ἄνθρωπος εἰς ψυχὴν ζῶσαν.*
>
> Then the Lord God formed man of dust from the ground, and breathed into his nostrils the breath of life; and man became a living being.

Genesis 2:7, understood in an EC context, makes a strong case that man does not share God's transcendence of nature, because the first man's origin was from the dirt. Literally this passage could be translated as follows:

63. White, "Continuing the Conversation," 60.

And (or, then) formed or fashioned[64] (וייצר, *wayîṣer*, Qal imperfect, masculine singular verb) יהוה אלהים, the Lord God . . . [65] Just as the name of God is different here than in the earlier creation account (1:26–28), the verb is different also. While נעשה (do, or make) used in the previous narrative is more reflective of an outcome—that something was made—the verb here connotes method more than does the other verb. The Greek verb ἔπλασεν (eplasen), meaning *to form, to mold,*[66] complements the Hebrew, and reinforces that the *forming* was from a preexisting material.

The object formed was את־האדם the man. While the earlier account referenced the creation of man and woman in an apparently collective sense, this account considers the creation of man independently from that of woman. This is contextually evident from the separate pericopes handling the creation of man and woman, respectively. Further, despite the accusative singular reference of the direct object in the LXX, as appears also in 1:27 (τὸν ἄνθρωπον), the structure of the passage requires the non-collective understanding of the term here.

The man is made of preexisting matter, namely עפר מן־האדמה (*apar min-ha 'ădamah*, dust from the ground). It is notable that no preposition (from) precedes עפר, thus the literal rendering is "And formed Yahweh Elohim the man the dust from the ground." The Hebrew implies an essential unity of man and dust—even insofar as their names are shared. The Greek χοῦν ἀπὸ τῆς γῆς (*choun apo tes ges*) retains the lack of preposition, likewise emphasizing the connection between man and dust. Rashi cites an interpretation that God gathered dust from the entire earth, so that wherever man may die, the earth would receive him for burial.[67] While this perspective exceeds the scope of the verbiage of 2:7, Rashi's is interesting in that it communicates the idea that man had an essential union with the entire earth. Man came from the dirt (2:7), he was charged to cultivate and keep the plants which grew from the same dirt (cf. 2:9 and 2:15), the fate of the dirt was directly connected to the fate of man (3:17), and the dirt would cooperate with man as long as he remained in his perfect inaugural condition (3:18). Any interpretation of the dominion mandate and man's relationship to nature must account for the first ingredient of the recipe for humanity.

64. BDB 427.

65. The distinctive reference to God as יהוה אלהים is carried over from 2:4, and represents a shift from the shorter form אלהים, appearing throughout chapter 1.

66. Lust et al, *Greek-English Lexicon*.

67. Ben Isaiah and Sharfman, *Pentateuch and Rashi's Commentary*, 20.

After forming man of the dust of the ground, God breathed (ויפח, *wayipaḥ* into his nostrils (באפיו, *bə 'apayw*, preposition with a dual noun and masculine suffix) the breath of life (נשמת חיים, *nišəmat ḥayiym*). As *breath* is in construct relationship to *life*, it is indicated that the breath referenced is not breath in the independent sense, but rather a particular *kind* of breath. The LXX renders this as a genitive relationship, πνοὴν ζωῆς (*pnoen zoes*), supporting the dependence of the breath on the life itself. Because man is endowed with the breath of life, whereas apparently the dust of the ground is not, the second ingredient seems to imbue man with at least some degree of transcendence of nature. It is on this idea that White seems to ground his critique that man shares God's transcendence over nature.

Whereas dominionism and stewardship both acqueiesce to the kind of transcendence White identifies, the citizenship view does not. Further, the Genesis narrative later acknowledges this same breath of life in animals (e.g., 7:15, 22), which adds more tension to the dominionism and stewarship interpretations. The only transcendence identified in the text thus far is by virtue of the *imago Dei*, not by any other essential component in mankind. If that image is augmented, diminished, or otherwise altered, then by consequence any transcendence is adjusted as well. This is a key point discussed in the analysis of Genesis 9, and one that tends against dominionism and stewardship, and in favor of redacted dominionism.

In summary, dominionism and stewardship represent within the EC two traditional approaches to interpreting the early Genesis data regarding the nature of mankind and the responsibilities that follow from that nature. Of the two, dominionism seems the most consistent with EC hermeneutic methodology applied to Genesis 1, but offers no seemingly viable grounding for environmental ethics, in that it does not consider human and nonhuman beings as having equitable value, and it is subject to accusations like those of White's (that it promulgates an anthropocentric cosmology). Further, as will be discussed in the next chapter, dominionism does not account for cosmological alterations from the Fall in Genesis 3. It is therefore not justified from the text itself, and it does not demonstrate a high degree of hermeneutic integrity. Dominionism, then, is ruled out here as being incapable of grounding a tenable biblical environmental ethic.

Stewardship, in contrast, does not account for the strong terminology of Genesis 1, and thus does not represent a very consistent application of EC methodology. While it does try to narrow the gap between the value of human and that of nonhuman beings, it does not go far enough to suitably resolve the gap. Consequently, stewardship is little more than a softer version of dominionism, and one that faces more severe challenges of inconsistency with especially the Genesis 1 account. Further, the stewardship interpretation does not exonerate the text from White's suspicions of anthropocentrism. As such, stewardship also at this point seems inadequate to ground a biblical environmental ethic.

Callicott's citizenship view, though the most novel of the three, is commendable for its crucial recognition that biblical descriptions of cosmology did not end in Genesis 2, and that the events in following narratives shape (and perhaps reshape) the man/nature relationship moving forward. Despite its worthiness in this regard, the citizenship view makes no attempt to reconcile with the language of the Genesis 1 mandate, thus disqualifying it as a potential solution for the EC.

Still, in considering the dramatic shift that takes place in Genesis 3, the citizenship interpretation foreshadows the possibility of an interpretation that accommodates both those changes as well as the earlier terminology of the first two chapters of Genesis. Redacted dominionism, as will be discussed in the next chapter, promises to account for both, thus providing the EC with a viable grounding for a biblical environmental ethic.

8

Value Theory in Genesis

THIS EXAMINATION OF THE biblical data of the early Genesis narrative begun in chapter 2 concludes with a consideration of Genesis chapters 3–9 and related contexts, which, according to the EC perspective, make profound statements regarding valuation of human and nonhuman beings. Consequently, the tone is set very early on in Genesis for grounding a biblical environmental ethic and warranting a discussion of a few aspects of value theory.

Also of note here in these chapters of Genesis is the announcement of cataclysmic changes that impact the ontological and functional value of human and nonhuman beings. Of the four views discussed here (dominionism, stewardship, citizenship, and redacted dominionism), each one handles the context as a whole with differing degrees of aplomb. After a brief consideration of the significance of value theory in the early Genesis narrative, and an explanation of the glory of God and the centrality of his doxological purpose, this chapter discusses the context of Genesis 3–9 and related passages, and concludes that redacted dominionism offers the best of the four views for grounding a biblical environmental ethic within EC methodology.

VALUE THEORY IN THE EARLY GENESIS NARRATIVE

J. Baird Callicott provides us a point of entry to the significance of value theory in the early Genesis narrative, noting that the central factors of the anthropocentric versus nonanthropocentric debate are rooted in value theory. He contrasts anthropocentric value theory, which primarily attributes intrinsic value to human life and only instrumental value to all nonhuman things, with nonanthropocentric value theory, which would also attribute intrinsic value to at least some nonhuman things.[1]

Here Callicott considers two broad axiological approaches to understanding human relations to nature, and he further identifies particular paradigms whereby a nonanthropocentric axiology can be derived for purposes of undergirding environmental ethics. He characterizes, for example, Jeremy Bentham's classic utilitarianism as nonanthropocentric in its basic structure, though he finds it inadequate for purposes of constructing an *environmental* ethic, because it limits the scope of moral consideration only to aspects of nature that are able to experience pleasure and pain. While the utilitarian principle would not necessarily create a man/nature dichotomy, it would promote a dichotomy between feeling and non-feeling beings.[2] Thus classic utilitarianism does not offer a suitable grounding for an environmental ethic that would comprehend for the whole of nature.

Callicott assesses the theistic axiology in its despotic interpretation as necessarily anthropocentric, though its stewardship interpretation is a paradigm measurably closer to nonanthropocentrism than its despotic counterpart. Nonetheless, the consistency problems inherent in the stewardship paradigm have been considered at length, especially in chapter 3 in comparing the creation accounts of Genesis 1 and 2, and Callicott likewise acknowledges the tension between the dominion imperatives of Genesis 1 and the stewardship interpretation. The appeal of the stewardship interpretation (for Callicott) is that, while conferring intrinsic value on humanity, it also seems to confer at least some intrinsic value on the world as a whole and on representative species therein.[3]

Despite the modest advantages of the stewardship model, Callicott finds the theistic axiology irreparably deficient in that it is "primitive, essentially mythic, ambiguous, and inconsistent with modern science."[4] He concludes that even the best theistic axiology does not offer a tenable solution to the problem, instead preferring "the Darwin-Leopold

1. Callicott "Non-Anthropocentric Value Theory," 299.
2. Jeremy Bentham, *Principles of Morals and Legislation*, 1:1.
3. Callicott, "Non-Anthropocentric Value Theory," 302.
4. Ibid.

environmental ethic, grounded in the axiology of Hume, on grounds that it can provide for the intrinsic value of non-human nature and is consistent with, and grounded in a contemporary scientific worldview."[5] In all this, Callicott parts company with the EC.

Whereas the despotic interpretation recognizes an essential dichotomy between man and nature, generally reckoning man to have intrinsic value while nature possesses merely instrumental value, Cal DeWitt, an advocate of "deep stewardship,"[6] attempts to close the gap between the human and nonhuman realms by attributing intrinsic value to nonhuman as well as human beings. He argues that in biblical Christianity the value of creatures is not instrumental but rather is intrinsic.[7] DeWitt suggests that value is derived not from use but from origin.

Like Callicott, DeWitt recognizes the need for a comprehensive value theory. DeWitt sees one emerging from the Genesis creation account. Specifically, because all nature (including mankind) has its origin in God, all nature possesses intrinsic value. DeWitt's conclusion, though, does not seem sufficiently to account for the dominion mandate nor for the *imago Dei* (a significant facet of distinction between humans and nonhuman nature). While the Genesis account may be interpreted as bestowing intrinsic value on all nature, clearly in any EC reading of Genesis, man is distinct from nature and would seem to possess more intrinsic value. Apparent inequity of value is unavoidable, even if intrinsic value is the device to be utilized. However, it is worth considering that intrinsic value is not a necessary quality in a nonanthropocentric value theory. Further, and perhaps more significantly, the early Genesis account never conclusively attributes intrinsic value to any created thing, but offers the possibility (at least within an EC understanding) that instrumental value is comprehensive. The account may even be understood to counter the inequality inherent in intrinsic value models of the despotic and stewardship interpretations of Genesis.

Notably, the Genesis 1 creation account concludes with the ascription that "God saw all that He had made and behold, it was very good" (Gen 1:31). While the intrinsic value of all nature may be justifiably asserted on the basis of this particular statement, it is equally possible that the passage assigns instrumental rather than intrinsic value to the whole

5. Ibid., 305.

6. Randolph and Yunt, "Cal DeWitt."

7. DeWitt, "Behemoth and Batrachians," 291–316.

of nature. Exegetically, from an EC evaluation of the passage and its immediate context, either interpretation would be textually justifiable. Further, all four models (despotism, stewardship, citizenship, and redacted dominionism) are plausible within an intrinsic value interpretation of Genesis 1:31, consequently this passage, so understood, is not pivotal in this discussion. However, if the passage is understood in context as referring to instrumental rather than intrinsic value, then the passage may provide additional support for redacted dominionism, in that the theocentric emphasis of redacted dominionism is more compatible with a comprehensive instrumental rather than intrinsic model.

The strongest biblical environmental ethic, at least in answering White's anthropocentric indictment, would provide both a comprehensive and an equitable axiology. An axiology that is comprehensive, applying to all created things, and is equitable, not axiologically elevating one created thing over another, is not subject to the anthropocentric problems White identifies. Rather such an axiology resolves the problem similarly to White's own prescription (by recommending a revitalization of the Christian tradition), only in the case of redacted dominionism it does so in a way that is tenable within the EC. Yet there are at least two possible types of comprehensively equitable ethics, those based on intrinsic value (as White and others support) and those based on instrumental value. The latter have advantages in that they align with the EC interpretations and, for all those people outside of the EC they avoid key challenges in the application of the ethic.

A comprehensively equitable ethic based on intrinsic value encounters significant contextual difficulties with justifying, for example, the killing of plants as food for humans (Gen 1:29) and in accounting for the *imago Dei* present in humanity but absent in the nonhuman realm. A comprehensively equitable ethic based on instrumental value would, however, resolve the practical difficulties associated with an anthropocentric moral ontology (consequently going a long way to defend the early Genesis narrative against the charge of anthropocentrism leveled by Leopold, McHarg, and White), and would favor, generally, a theocentric perspective.

The practical value of the theocentric instrumentalism model proposed here is that it allows for infringement of other species, but only insofar as permitted by God. For example, God permitted the human consumption of nonhuman living things (Gen 9:3), but disallowed the consumption of those creatures with their blood (or presumably, while they were still alive; see Gen 9:4). Further, because the instrumental value of created things is not biblically quantified, using it as a foundation for environmental ethics may lessen the temptation for mankind to uncover a hierarchy in nature, and instead understand that theocentric instrumentalism means that all things are useful in their own way for expressing and illustrating the glory of God. The Apostle Paul illustrates this principle of value within the context of the importance of varying human roles when he says, " . . . even as the body is one and yet has many members . . . though they are many, are one body . . . But now God has placed the members, each one of them, in the body, just as He desired" (1 Cor 12:12,18). In Paul's illustration, function and value are unrelated: "And if the ear should say, 'Because I am not an eye, I am not a part of the body,' it is not for this reason any the less a part of the body" (1 Cor 12:16). Though Paul's illustration describes human relations to Christ and to one another, the principle can be borrowed to illustrate human relations to nature. Theocentric instrumentalism does not deny ontological inequity between human and nonhuman beings, but it does assert that this inequity has no implications for the instrumental value of all creatures. Just as the most seemingly insignificant part of the human body is still a part of the body, even so the most seemingly insignificant part of nature still has its place in God's program.

In either case, due to the relevance of value theory to the present discussion, what is intended by the divine proclamation of goodness is significant. If intrinsic value is intended then intrinsic value *is not* the sufficient condition for functional equality in nature, as the dominion mandate is given just prior to the alleged acknowledgment of universal possession of intrinsic value. In other words, the intrinsic value of nature is not sufficient to keep it from being suborned and governed by mankind.

The text itself can be interpreted as supporting the idea that the value acknowledged by the divine proclamation of approval is instrumental rather than intrinsic. Genesis 1–2 identifies no purpose for God's creative work, nor does the remainder of Genesis, though we do find in Genesis some clues about man's value in God's eyes. No amount of intrinsic value in man and nature stopped God from proclaiming, "I will blot out man whom I have created from the face of the land, from man to animals to creeping things and to birds of the sky . . . " (6:7). In this context, there is no axiological distinction between human and nonhuman. Nor did God characterize man as having intrinsic value when he declared that "the intent of man's heart is evil from his youth" (8:21). And while the murder prohibition invokes the *imago Dei* as the warrant for retributive justice (9:6), the debt may be understood as owed to God on occasion of violating his image, rather than as owed to man because of intrinsic value.

Broadening the context of the examination beyond the immediate scope of Genesis, we may observe that Psalm 19:1–6 indicates the heavens, heavenly bodies, and even the measurement of time all serve one basic purpose: to declare the glory of God. Isaiah 40 emphasizes his transcendence over humanity and all of created nature, indicating, "All the nations are as nothing before Him, They are regarded by Him as less than nothing and meaningless" (Isa 40:17), and the earth's "inhabitants are like grasshoppers" (Isa 40:22). Any special standing humanity may enjoy seems not to be grounded on the basis of human intrinsic value (Isaiah 40, for example, de-emphasizes human intrinsic value), but rather on the basis that the goings on of the natural world ultimately reveal God's glory (Isa 40:5). On the face of it, the value of humanity, in this context, is in its contribution to the demonstration of God's glory.

Further, Job 38–39 recounts God's response to Job's questioning of God's role in the tragic events of Job's life. After hearing God's handling of Job's self-centered questions, Job can only respond, "Behold, I am insignificant; what can I reply to Thee?" (40:4). Likewise, Psalm 89:11 characterizes the heavens and earth and all they contain as belonging to God on the basis that God created them. This concept of sovereign rights by virtue of creation is later illustrated by the Apostle Paul in Romans 9:21, when he asks, " . . . does not the potter have a right over the clay, to make from the same lump one vessel for honorable use, and another for common use?"

Thus, in an EC interpretation, God can be understood as the creator who has sovereign rights over creation. This understanding invites the relevant question of why God created in the first place. According to the EC, the Hebrew Bible (HB) asserts the purpose as the expression of God's glory, and the Greek New Testament (NT) concurs. Consider the observations of Paul in Ephesians 1: the predestining work of God is not based on the value of those being predestined, but rather on the "intention of His will" (1:5). Once again, intrinsic value (if there is any) seems de-emphasized. Again, his "intention" is referenced in 1:9 and is asserted to be purposed in "the fullness of the times . . . the summing up of all things . . . things in the heavens and things upon the earth" (1:10). The intention is for the summing up of all things, but to what end? The ultimate goal is "To the praise of the glory of His grace" (1:16), and "To the praise of His glory" (1:12–13). The NT teaching is consistent with and confirms the HB teaching on the matter: (1) God created everything; (2) over that which God created, God has sovereign rights; and (3) the only stated purpose of God's creative work is ultimately a doxological one.[8]

If this is a viable understanding of God's purpose in creating, then whether or not man and nature have intrinsic value is irrelevant (it may also be indiscernible). In any case, while certainly value in general is discernible in the text, intrinsic value is not. In fact, the only value that is biblically discernable with any degree of certainty is that all of nature—human and nonhuman alike—possesses instrumental value to God. Perhaps the impact such an assertion would have on environmental ethics is readily apparent: if God has sovereign rights as the creator and created all things to serve a doxological purpose, then each individual aspect of creation serves no other (identified) purpose than to serve God's purpose, and thus any infringement of one natural element against another—whether human or nonhuman—would qualify as a direct offense to God.

Therefore, humans can infringe on specimens only insofar as permitted by God, and only in consideration of doxological rather than anthropocentric purpose. This assertion is echoed by the Apostle Paul, who later writes in 1 Corinthians 10:31, "Whatever, then, you eat or drink or whatever you do, do all to the glory of God." A theocentric perspective has the added advantage of motivating humanity to a much less selfish existence in which we would be unwilling to abuse and even destroy the "kinds" (Gen 1:21) around us. A doxological perspective would not require that eating another animal be viewed as inappropriate, for example, but to exhibit cruelty (Prov 12:10), to be excessive (Luke 12:15; Eph 5:3), and to be broadly and inconsiderately destructive (Ezek 34:18–19) would be unacceptable. Further, to infringe upon species or kinds to the point (i.e., extinction) at which they are unable to obey their own "Be fruitful and multiply" imperative (as found in Gen 1:22) is hardly compatible with a doxological perspective.

The debt, then, incurred by irresponsibility—ecological or other—is owed to God, and not to any aspect of the creation itself, as Abraham Kuyper eloquently enunciates,

8. This is to identify the purpose as expressing or illustrating God's glory.

> Not we have made the world, and thus in our sin we have not maltreated an art product of our own. No, that world was the contrivance, the work and the creation of the Lord our God. It was and is His world, which belonged to Him, which He had created for His glory, and for which we with that world were by Him appointed. Not to us did it belong, but to Him. It was His. And His divine world we have spoiled and corrupted.[9]

Again, if this interpretation of biblical data pertaining to value is viable, then the question of intrinsic value can thus be dismissed as the central issue in the debate. This move is advantageous on several accounts. First, because there are no explicit biblical quantifications of the apparently unequal intrinsic value of creatures, human or nonhuman, precision in discerning actual intrinsic value within an EC framework is for all intents and purposes, impossible. In fact it seems far more likely that no created thing possesses any intrinsic value at all but instead only possesses instrumental value to God. Even if this latter point is an overstatement, the former is not, and as a result, consensus is unlikely.

Second, acknowledging even the highest degree of intrinsic value to nonhuman components of nature does not account fully for the metaphysical dichotomy that the *imago Dei* suggests to the EC, nor would it resolve the tension that results from the understanding that, as White puts it, man is one thing and nature is another. Thus it does not lend itself to a stronger biblical ethic that is both comprehensive and equitable. Third, the text, understood within an EC context, simply does not support the discussion of intrinsic value with any clear assertions, though the text is fairly explicit about the instrumental value of all creation.

Finally, rejecting intrinsic value in favor of instrumental value resolves the problem Werther anticipates when he considers the implication that functional superiority implies ontological superiority. He poses the problem as follows: "One might think that if humanity is to play a special role in God's creation, then there must be something special about humanity. If humans are to rule over the work of 'God's hands,' then it is plausible to think that humans are not only different in kind than the rest of God's creation but ontologically superior as well."[10] In Werther's problem, one's function is determined at least to some extent by one's degree of value. While intrinsic value need not be equitable to be

9. Kuyper, *Keep Thy Solemn Feasts*, 70–71.

10. Werther, "Reason and the Imago Dei," 326–27.

comprehensive, Werther recognizes the inherent inequality of a biblical, intrinsic value model that does justice to all the elements of the text.

This is the basic dilemma for claims of biblical intrinsic value: if function may be determined biblically primarily by intrinsic value (Werther), and if intrinsic value is not quantified in the Bible, then perhaps differences in function cannot be biblically ascertained either. Instead, in recognizing that all aspects of nature have the same instrumental value there is no axiological distinction between human and nonhuman, even if there may be a metaphysical one. This model allows for the retaining of a possible metaphysical distinction without positing an axiological distinction that would result in *de facto* anthropocentrism. Nonanthropocentric instrumentalism, or doxological instrumentalism is compatible with an EC reading of the biblical data, and offers grounding for a comprehensive (broadly applicable) and equitable (recognizing that all species have an equal quality of value in God's sight) environmental ethic.[11]

THE GLORY OF GOD AND THE CENTRALITY OF THE DOXOLOGICAL PURPOSE

At this point, some brief definition and discussion of the glory of God is needed in order to help clarify the relationship of God's glory to a biblical environmental ethic—and specifically to redacted dominionism. The glory of God is an unmistakably significant theme in the Hebrew Bible, and a critical component of a theocentric cosmology in which all created things have instrumental value to God. The English word *glory* often evokes images of self-aggrandizement and vanities that seem inconsistent with what one might expect in God's character as a superior and considerate being who might care even a little bit about what is done with the earth.

The term usually translated as *glory* from the HB, כבד (*kebod)*, is understood to reference honor, splendor, or magnitude.[12] The Greek counterpart appearing in the LXX is *δόξα* (*doxa*), understood in a subjective sense as the opinion that others have of the subject, and in an objective

11. Doxological is a theocentric perspective, focusing on God's purpose of expressing his own glory.

12. BDB 458.

sense as the magnificence of the subject.[13] EC and non-EC Bible scholars alike generally consider the glorification of God as equivalent to "I will declare His beauty."[14] EC theologian Paul Enns asserts that the beauty of the heavens and earth "reflect the glory of God."[15] Enns's description is helpful in that it emphasizes that God is not trying to get glory, but is rather demonstrating the glory he already possesses. From the nearly two hundred appearances of the term (glory) in the HB, it seems that the glory of God connotes the idea of *self-expression of his beauty*. As the Apostle Paul later acknowledges, " . . . since the creation of the world, His invisible attributes, His eternal power, and divine nature have been clearly seen, being understood through what was made . . . " (Rom 1:19). God's interaction within and involving all that is created may be understood (and is so by the EC, at least) as the expression of his character. This idea is consistent with the self-expressive creativity of humanity as perhaps an aspect of the *imago Dei*.

If the glory of God may be described as in the foregoing paragraph, then the centrality of the doxological purpose in the Bible may be fairly easy to ascertain. The term *doxological*, a compound of *doxa* (glory) and *logos* (word or idea), is a theological term to communicate something that acknowledges the glory of God. The doxological purpose of God is that strong undercurrent in the Bible explicitly proposing that God's purpose in creating and working within his creation is the self-expression of his beauty, magnificence, character, etc.—the expression of his glory. This is no insignificant theme, but rather is central not only to the HB, but also to the NT (e.g., in thematic order: Ps 86:9–10; Rev 15:4; Eph 1:5–12; 2 Pet 1:3; John 13:31–32; 17:1–5; 21:19; 2 Cor 1:21; Heb 12:21; Ps 19; Isa 40; Rev 4:11; Rom 3:1–7; Ps 79:9; Rom 15:7; 16:25–27; Eph 1:14; 1 Tim 1:15–17; 2 Tim 4:18; Jude 24–25; 1 Cor 10:31; 2 Cor 4:15; Eph 1:12; Phil 1:11; 2 Thess 1:11–12; 1 Pet 4:11, 16; John 15:8; Phil 2:11; 1 Thess 2:12; Rev 1:6; 1 Sam 6:5; Luke 17:11–18; John 9:1–3; 11:4; Rev 14:7; Isa 25:1–3; 43:20; 60:21; 61:3; Luke 2:14; Rom 4:20; 15:8–9; 2 Cor 1:20; 2 Pet 1:3–4; Rev 19:7).

If God's purpose in creating and working within creation may be understood as doxological (expressing his own character, beauty, or glory), then a theocentric cosmology might come as no surprise to the biblical

13. Lust et al, *Greek-English Lexicon*.

14. Ben Isaiah and Sharfman, *Pentateuch and Rashi's Commentary*, 153.

15. Enns, *Moody Handbook of Theology*, 205.

interlocutor. Human and nonhuman nature could be understood, in this interpretive matrix, to possess the same quality of value (instrumental rather than intrinsic) even if the quantity of that value might be difficult to apprehend. The anthropocentrism that Leopold, McHarg, and White perceive of Western Christianity could be regarded then as incompatible with a theocentric model, because the anthropocentric model to which they allude seems to view things as serving human rather than divine purposes.[16] In fact, the anthropocentric purpose is the central concept that White condemns and suggests replacing, although his assumption that it is possible to do only by rejecting the narrative of Genesis is neither necessary nor acceptable to the EC. The theocentric principle discussed here can be a cornerstone for a strong biblical environmental ethic. Redacted dominionism builds, with EC interpretive methodology, on the theocentric premise, agreeing with White that the anthropocentric model is deficient and must be replaced.

16. White, "Historical Roots," 1207.

9

Considering Genesis 3–9

RETURNING NOW TO THE Genesis context, we recall that Genesis 1:26–28 includes a dominion mandate, and one that was linked to the creation of humanity in the image of God. The verb רדה, translated by the NASB as rule, does not imply *prima facie* the idea of stewardship. It seems appropriately translated as rule or dominate. This dominion mandate was given to pre-Fall mankind who was qualified through the *imago Dei* as God's representative to properly govern the earth. Generations of dominionists since have seemingly failed to consider the impact of the events soon following. As mankind was created in the image of God, God declares that his creation, including mankind, was very good (1:31). But the sin of Genesis 3 resulted in a changed condition for mankind and all of creation. Mankind was no longer qualified to govern creation, as evidenced by (1) the curse that came to the earth as a result of Adam's (poorly undertaken) dominion (3:17); through (2) increased difficulty in working with the earth (3:17–18); by (3) a finite and shortened human lifespan that would make knowledge of nature far more difficult to obtain, even if only because humans would have less time to accumulate such knowledge (3:19); and most importantly, (4) the image of God in mankind was now altered or augmented by the image of Adam—of a man no longer bearing, untarnished, the qualification to govern the earth as God's representative (5:3). The only textually cited qualification (the untarnished *imago Dei*) for mankind to govern was altered, and human influence on creation subsequently resulted in a curse.

Genesis 3:22 recounts a brief consideration by God regarding the scope of judgment to be executed on humanity. Already, death was promised, but if the man and woman remained in the garden they might perhaps partake of the tree of life—which would allow them immortality without any consideration of regeneration or rehabilitation. Notably, in this brief commentary God speaks in the first person plural (us). While at first glance, this may raise questions regarding whether he is speaking of angels or perhaps other deities (the latter of which could offer an alternative narrative as to why the doxological purpose is central in the biblical writers—to express superiority over those other deities), we can recall an identical use of the first person plural in 1:26, and its resolution to the emphatic third person singular in 1:27. Just as happens in 1:26–27, the narrative quickly returns to the third person singular in 3:23–24. Whereas Judaic commentators (e.g., Rashi[1]) consider this syntactical maneuver to be reflective of conversation had with angels, the EC understands it to be a reinforcement of the plurality of persons in the godhead (similar to the reinforcement of plurality perceived by the EC in Deuteronomy 6:4 and Isaiah 48:12 and 16). In any case, God's judgment—the death promised in Genesis 2:17—is so final and thorough as to necessitate the removal of the man and woman from any possibility for divinely unaided and ordained appropriation of eternal life.

God's subsequent description of human quality sounds nothing like an endorsement of human qualification for governing the earth: "Then the Lord saw that the wickedness of man was great on the earth, and that every intent of the thoughts of his heart was only evil continually" (Gen 6:5). If there was a dominion mandate, man had failed miserably at following it, yet because no new mandate to replace the first one was given at this juncture, it would appear that man was still attempting to function in a sovereign role, though lacking the qualification and ability to do it successfully.

To return for a moment to the intrinsic-value question and the accusation of biblical anthropocentrism by its environmental critics, the indictment of 6:13 shows a decidedly theocentric rather than anthropocentric perspective on God's part, as God says to Noah, " . . . the earth is filled with violence because of them; and behold I am about to destroy them with the earth." Man was not too sacred to be destroyed along with other creatures and with even the land itself. Evident here is an axiological

1. Ben Isaiah and Sharfman, *Pentateuch and Rashi's Commentary*, 14.

equality between human, animal, and land. This judgment challenges the idea that humanity uniquely possesses intrinsic value while other elements of nature have only instrumental value. At first it appears that by virtue of humanity's unique relation to the *imago Dei* mankind possesses a degree of intrinsic value shared by no other created thing. But this conclusion appears premature in light of God's responses to pre and post-Fall humanity.

First, in consideration of God's interaction with pre-Fall humanity, Genesis 2:16–17 records the prohibition of human eating from the tree of the knowledge of good and evil. It is worth noting here that the use of the word *knowledge* might imply a paradox (how could Adam and Eve have known that eating of the tree was evil if they didn't already have knowledge of evil?), but the Hebrew הדעת (*ha da'at*, translated *the knowledge*) is the same root used in Genesis 4:1, to connote the act of Adam's intimate knowledge of Eve. In other words, these seem to refer not merely to conceptual knowledge (which Adam and Eve would have needed in order to understand the prohibition), but rather to a kind of knowledge that was gained through experience of the subject.

The LXX helps to clarify as in the Greek there are several words connoting knowledge, yet in both of these instances the LXX uses the root γνῶσις (*gnosis*) to indicate that experiential knowledge is the intended understanding. Still, not all EC interpreters agree that experiential knowledge is in view. EC Bible scholar Bruce Waltke for example, suggests that this refers to comprehensive knowledge, and that without the comprehensive knowledge that the tree would offer, Adam and Eve could not speak absolutely about what was good or evil.[2] In either case, experiential and comprehensive knowledge can be distinguished from the conceptual knowledge that the man and woman may be supposed to have had at the time the prohibition was given.[3] Still, more directly to the point at hand, the initial man and woman, even in a state of sinlessness, did not share God's comprehensive (at least) knowledge of good and evil, and the prohibition regarding the tree implies that God did not intend for man to ascertain in any comprehensive (or experiential, perhaps) way "the work which God has done from the beginning even to the end" (Eccl 3:11).

2. Waltke, *Genesis*, 46.

3. Note Callicott's arguments that the knowledge here pertains neither to sexual awareness or the general knowledge that it would be wrong to disobey the imperative. Callicott, *Beyond the Land Ethic*, 208.

The knowledge of good and evil, Callicott suggests, refers to "the power to judge, to decide, to determine what is good and what is evil in relation so self . . . once aware of themselves, they may treat themselves as an axiological point of reference."[4] He bases this interpretation, consistent with EC methodology, on a literal reading of the text. The only specific knowledge that the text says that Adam and Eve acquired was that they knew they were naked. Callicott takes Adam's and Eve's knowledge of their nakedness (Gen 3:7) to be an indication of a newly acquired self-awareness. He adds, "once aware of themselves they will inevitably treat themselves as an intrinsic hub to which other creatures and the creation as a whole may be referred for appraisal."[5] In short, Callicott's suggestion is that the original sin is anthropocentrism, and is a conclusion wholly compatible with EC methodology. At least it is clear that Adam and Eve exalted themselves over and against God by abandoning his prescriptions in favor of alternate self-centered machinations.

So then, pre-Fall humanity was limited (despite the *imago Dei*)—and designedly so. The Fall, it seems, represented an attempt on the part of humanity to surpass those limits, much like the one who declared, "I will ascend to heaven; I will raise my throne above the stars of God . . . I will make myself like the Most High" (Isa 14:13–14). Further, God's interaction with pre-Fall humanity reinforces the reality of that limitation, and consequently a reinforcement of the idea that inaugural mankind did not share God's kind of transcendence over creation.

Likewise, God's interaction with post-Fall humanity indicates at least two elements germane especially to the despotic interpretation: (1) a change in human qualification and ability to govern creation, and (2) occasion to see that human value is not so distinct from the rest of creation that mankind can be said to have intrinsic value while the remainder of nature has merely instrumental value.

The sin of Genesis 3 resulted in a changed condition for humanity and all creation (3:14–19). Human dominion was a failure that brought a curse for all creation, and the forthcoming labors of mankind in working with the earth would be, as a result, increasingly difficult (3:17). Mankind would have a finite lifespan that would further inhibit discovery of and fruitfulness in nature, since humanity would have less time to gain knowledge of nature (3:19). Still, the most significant cost of sin was

4. Ibid.

5. Ibid., 9.

the tarnishing of the *imago Dei* with the new image of Adam (5:3). This ontological change came with a pronouncement contrasting the Genesis 1:31 declaration that it was all "very good." Instead, "the Lord saw that the wickedness of man was great on the earth and that every intent of the thoughts of his heart was only evil continually" (6:5).

Incidentally, the downward spiral evident in Genesis 1–11 does not lend credence to the idea that humanity maintains any present qualification for dominion—especially since the only textually cited condition for human qualification for governance was the untarnished *imago Dei*. In other areas (such as spiritual condition and ethical ability), the EC acknowledges that the tarnishing of the *imago Dei* left mankind unqualified. In fact the Reformed doctrine of human depravity,[6] adopted in principle by many (though not all) in the EC, acknowledges that from the moment of original sin mankind became an enemy of God. As the Apostle Paul explains the post-Fall human condition, "you were dead in your trespasses and sins . . . having no hope and without God in the world" (Eph 2:1, 12).

The indictment of 6:13, that man was to be destroyed with the other creatures, shows a decidedly nonanthropocentric, and indeed a theocentric perspective on God's part. The judgment implies that humanity was not above nature, but was rather considered by God to be a part of it. It seems humanity was judged, in part, based on a failure to relate properly to the created world.[7] Further, Genesis 7:15 describes all living things as having the breath (spirit) of life. This provides yet another support for the at least some kind of equality of all living things.

After the judgment of Genesis 6–8, humanity was to go forth with the same simple purpose as that of all other living things: proliferation (8:17). Post-Fall conditions were not repaired to pre-Fall glory (8:21). In order for humanity to simply survive, special accommodations were introduced, including a murder prohibition (9:6), and the fear of man placed in animals (9:2, 5). No longer was humanity qualified or equipped to dominate, or even to steward, thus the dominion and stewardship

6. As John Calvin puts it, "the dominion of sin, from the time it held the first man bound to itself, not only ranges among all mankind, but completely occupies individual souls . . . he is said to have no ability to pursue righteousness on his own." Calvin, *Institutes of the Christian Religion*, 255.

7. The account of the original human sin indicates humanity had direction about how and how not to interact with the created world (specifically, the fruit of certain trees could be eaten, whereas, others could not [2:16–17]). Interestingly, the first human failure involved a misappropriation of nature.

interpretations are challenged in resolving tensions between the dominion mandate of 1:26–28 and the proliferation mandates of 8:15—9:7. Most notably, 9:7 repeats verbatim the mandate of 1:28 in all respects but that it excludes the dominion aspect.

GENESIS 8:15—9:6—DOMINIONISM, STEWARDSHIP, AND CITIZENSHIP: CONSIDERING POST-FALL CONDITIONS

As Genesis 6–8 recounts God's judgment on man, animal, and environment, the events immediately following shed light on the two aforementioned major issues emerging from the Fall. First, in 8:17 appears another instance of functional equality between human and nonhuman beings: "bring out with you every living thing of all flesh . . . that they may breed abundantly on the earth, and be fruitful and multiply on the earth." The phrase concluding verse 17 (על־הארץ ורבו ופרו) is very similar to the first subset of imperatives of 1:28, and includes in this context both human and nonhuman beings (cf. 8:16–17 and 8:18–19). Mankind was to go out from the ark with the same stated purpose as nonhuman: reproduction and species population increase. Second, the post-Fall human condition is not repaired to its pre-Fall glory: "the intent of man's heart is evil from his youth" (8:21), but instead it remains as it was initially after the Fall and pre-flood (cf. 6:5 and 8:21). Thus any qualification and ability that was lost in the Fall remained lost even post-flood. In order for man even to survive, God installs a sanctity-of-life ethic (i.e., capital punishment, 9:6), and further, God places the fear of man in animals so that they might not destroy mankind (9:2, 5).[8]

While these verses confirm man's change in qualification and ability and confirm at least functional equality between man and nature, 8:15—9:6 provide an additional important contribution. That God adjusts the natural world to protect humans from nonhuman beings, but not to protect nonhuman beings, implies that the metaphysical distinction between the two groups has not been eradicated. Man and nature are not ontologically the same (importantly, metaphysical distinctions are irrelevant to instrumental value). The *imago Dei* remains (9:6), though it has

8. The context is considering the survival of mankind, and the accountability of animals for the blood of humanity. Thus while it seems that animal fear of humanity would serve to help protect animals against abuses by humanity, the context is more directly addressing human protection against human and nonhuman threats.

been augmented by a fallen image (5:3). Thus man bears enough of the *imago Dei* to keep him distinct from the remainder of the natural world, but that image is tarnished sufficiently to keep man from the qualification and ability to govern the world.

If this interpretation is viable, then legitimate challenges to the dominionist, stewardship, and citizenship views are apparent. That there remains a metaphysical distinction between human and nonhuman challenges the citizenship understanding, which views people as "created to be a part of, not set apart from, nature."[9] That the qualification facilitated by the unaugmented *imago Dei* to oversee nature in some way has been lost by virtue of Adam's trespass offers a significant contextual problem for both the dominionist and stewardship views. In light of these two considerations, the stewardship view seems to come the closest to addressing the problems, because practically speaking, stewardship does relate human qualification to steward creation as deriving from the *imago Dei*. Still, problems remain, namely, the incompatibility of stewardship with the initial despotic mandate (1:26–28), and ultimately the absence within the text itself of any discernible post-Fall dominion or stewardship mandate.

GENESIS 9:7—REDACTED DOMINIONISM IS A PLAUSIBLE ALTERNATIVE

> וְאַתֶּ֖ם פְּר֣וּ וּרְב֑וּ שִׁרְצ֥וּ בָאָ֖רֶץ וּרְבוּ־בָֽהּ׃
>
> *ὑμεῖς δὲ αὐξάνεσθε καὶ πληθύνεσθε καὶ πληρώσατε τὴν γῆν καὶ πληθύνεσθε ἐπ̓ αὐτῆς.*
>
> As for you, be fruitful and multiply; Populate the earth abundantly and multiply in it.

The accommodations made in 8:15—9:7 and the universal aspects discussed in 9:12–16[10] are indicative that God did not plan all of nature explicitly for man's benefit and rule, but rather for his own. It is notable that God actively places limits on his own and on human activity in order for the continual existence and function of nature (cf. 8:21 and 9:4), and ultimately for his own benefit. In light of these characteristics along with

9. Callicott, *Beyond the Land Ethic*, 217.

10. The covenant is repeatedly referenced as being made not just with humanity, but also with every living creature.

the broad context of the early Genesis narratives, at least considered in an EC context, suggestions (such as that of White) that Christianity is the world's most anthropocentric religion are not supported by the theocentric themes of the early Genesis narrative which imply that anthropocentrism is not a proper possibility, at least within an EC understanding of Genesis.

Genesis 9:7 includes the second person plural pronoun, ואתם, coupled with four second person plural imperatives: (1) פרו—you be fruitful (αὐξάνεσθε in the LXX), (2) ורבו—and you become many or great (πληθύνεσθε in the LXX), (3) שרצו בארץ—you swarm or teem in the land (πληρώσατε τὴν γῆν in the LXX), and (4) שרצו בארץ—and become many or great in it (πληθύνεσθε ἐπ αὐτῆς in the LXX). The first two imperatives are identical to the first two commands of 1:28 in both the BHS and LXX. The third is slightly altered in the BHS, and the fourth appears to replace the dominion mandate entirely. In a consistent application of EC principles, *the new cultural mandate for mankind and for all of nature may be understood simply as the proliferation of the species.* Still, not all interlocutors accept the replacement of the old one.

Richard Wright, an EC environmental scholar, in arguing that the dominion mandate remains the consistent representation of the Bible, indicates that "The injunction is repeated to Noah after the flood story and is recognized by David, writing in the 8th Psalm."[11] Yet, if the Genesis narrative is examined through any kind of literalistic hermeneutic, there is found no such repetition to Noah. Still, if there can be discovered an acknowledgment of the dominion mandate as prescriptive for post-Fall generations (as Wright suggests is found in Psalm 8), then the absence of the mandate in the Noahic injunctions becomes far less significant. Despite Wright's assertion, however, in the immediate context of Genesis it may be understood, within an EC framework, that dominion is no longer the intent, and that dominion is no longer even possible considering the conditions and the allowances made by God for basic human survival. In fact, further accommodations are needed even beyond those of 9:1–6. God covenants with all living things (9:12) that he will not again judge the world by flood (9:11).

Some argue, as do evangelical theologians Lewis and Demarest, on theological grounds that man's post-Fall condition is restored to its pre-Fall glory by virtue of individual salvation and the efforts of God

11. Wright, "Responsibility for the Ecological Crisis," 851.

in regeneration.[12] While there may be some viability in the statement (the NT does claim that the Spirit's work of regeneration brings renewed spiritual capabilities), there is no textual grounding in any biblical context that the *imago Dei* is affected one way or the other by individual regeneration. In fact, besides simply restating that man was made in the image of God, the Bible is entirely silent on the issue, thus there seems no exegetical warrant to suggest that the consequences of the Fall are entirely removed at present.

Ultimately, the presumption that the dominion mandate applies to fallen man is exegetically unwarranted (again, within EC hermeneutic framework), and results in a dangerous kind of anthropocentrism—the like of which White and others decry. It seems folly, to this writer, to presume that humanity can redeem creation when humanity is itself in need of redemption. Perhaps it is this kind of arrogance that White and other critics sense when they encounter proponents of the biblical accounts who argue for human dominion. Ironically, in holding to dominion as the present condition, despotic interpreters find themselves situating humanity in a role that seems reserved for God alone—as master, possessor, and redeemer of creation.

Perhaps it is this kind of anthropocentrism that causes White and others to bristle. While White's criticisms do not necessarily square with the early Genesis narrative, he certainly seems to offer one poignant diagnosis: anthropocentrism is a major part of the problem, as mankind's self-exaltation has had only dismal results.

12. Lewis and Demarest assert, "The Spirit's work of regeneration renews the heart (spirit), restoring the use of all one's debilitated spiritual capabilities. The imago Dei, impaired and enslaved by the Fall, is rejuvenated." Lewis and Demarest, *Integrative Theology*, 105.

10

Conclusion: An Objection and a Proposal

CONSIDERING PSALM 8 AS A POSSIBLE OBJECTION

WHILE THE DOMINION IMPERATIVE is not repeated to post-Fall humanity Genesis, Wright's suggestion that Psalm 8, one of few passages—and perhaps the most significant —outside of Genesis that addresses human value, is evidence of enduring human dominion and underscores the need for examining the Psalm. For perhaps the Psalmist can offer some interpretive insight on the value theory addressed in Genesis. As discussed earlier, the rule and subdue imperatives of Genesis 1:26–28, understood in an EC interpretive model, should be understood in light of the ontological-condition changes of Genesis 3 and the redacted imperative of 9:7.

Psalm 8:4–8 reads:

> What is man, that Thou dost take thought of him? And the son of man, that Thou dost care for him? Yet Thou hast made him a little lower than God. And dost crown him with glory and majesty! Thou dost make him to rule over the works of Thy hands; Thou hast put all things under his feet, All sheep and oxen, And also the beasts of the field, The birds of the heavens, and the fish of the sea, Whatever passes through the paths of the seas.

The passage is often understood to be an interpretive aid to the Genesis 1 account, usually with the assumption that it represents the prevailing human condition as understood by the Psalmist. Biblical commentator Abraham Cohen takes this view, suggesting Psalm 8 indicates, "The human being is on a far higher plane . . . the king of the terrestrial sphere."[1] Frank Gaebelein adds, "Man is God's appointed governor (vassal) over creation . . . to maintain dominion over creation."[2] Keil and Delitzsch assert that "Man is a king, and not a king without a territory; the world around . . . is his kingdom."[3]

While this despotic reading is the most popular interpretation, there are two alternative interpretations of considerable importance. First, the Hebrew verb תמשילהו (*amašîlēhû*), translated *rule* in the NASB is the hiphil (causative) imperfect of the root משל, which though not the same term used in Genesis 1 dominion mandate, indicates *ruling, having dominion,* or *reigning.*[4] The imperfect tense can denote incomplete action or even future action, thus the syntax can allow for an interpretation of the verbal phrase, as God will cause man to have dominion. This could thus speak of an interrupted process (God created man to have dominion, but it is not presently a completed process), an understanding not inconsistent with the creation account and the change of condition resulting in the modified cultural mandate. This interpretation understands mankind, though referenced in the singular, as collectively one day to have a restored dominion.

The second alternative to a reiteration of an ongoing dominion mandate is the interpretation of the NT writer of the book of Hebrews, who quotes the passage from the LXX, and applies it not to mankind in general, but to one man in particular: Jesus (cf. Heb 2:5–8 and 2:9). Even if the singular αὐτοῦ in Hebrews 2:8 (quoting the LXX, Ps 8:7) were to be understood as collectively referencing humanity rather than an individual, the writer concludes the verse by indicating that functional superiority is not a present reality. Thus either Psalm 8 is referencing one individual's future functional superiority or the collective's future functional superiority, and in neither case is there presently a functional superiority. If the Hebrews author's interpretation is to be accepted here (as it could be in

1. A. Cohen, *Psalms*, 19.
2. F. Gaebelein, *Expositor's Bible Commentary*, 114.
3. Keil and Delitzsch, *Commentary on the Old Testament*, 5:94.
4. BDB 605.

EC methodology)—that man and the following pronouns are intended in the singular and non-collective sense—then Psalm 8 is understood to be messianic,[5] and does not offer any commentary on collective mankind's ontological or functional value. If this were the case, then Psalm 8 would not be interpreted as justifying present human functional superiority.

If the collective use is indeed the one intended, then the primary issue at stake in Psalm 8 is the nature of man's ontological value and the relation between ontological and functional value. Consider the following argument:

> P1: Humans are ontologically superior to nonhuman creatures.
>
> P2: Functional superiority is derived from ontological superiority.
>
> C: Thus, humans have functional superiority over nonhuman creatures.

This argument assumes the collective αὐτοῦ (*of him*), and consequently accepts the positive truth-value of P1. P2 is grounded in the phrase, "And dost crown him with glory and majesty!" The conclusion follows that mankind therefore has functional superiority, and more specifically, is to rule over all of nature. It also assumes that the functional superiority is an ongoing reality. If the collective pronoun is not in view, then P1 must be restructured. Likewise, if the writer of Hebrews interprets the tense correctly, then P1 must be reconsidered. The argument can also be represented in the reverse form:

> P1: Humans have functional superiority over nonhuman creatures.
>
> P2: Functional superiority is derived from ontological superiority.
>
> C: Thus, humans have ontological superiority over nonhuman creatures.

In this form P1 also assumes the collective pronoun does not consider the Hebrews commentary, thus the problems with P1 in both arguments are substantial. Further, in both forms of the argument P2 is assumed, but not justified.

David Werther raises another problem for present functional superiority from the text of Psalm 8, challenging the premise that functional

5. Prophetically anticipating the advent of the Messiah.

superiority is derived from essential or ontological superiority.[6] Assuming Werther's premise of angelic ontological superiority over humanity (as derived from Psalm 8:5a), then human ontological superiority over animals would not directly imply human functional superiority over animals.

While it seems that the writer of Hebrews offers the most plausible means of understanding that Psalm 8 is not an indicator of collective man's functional value, there are other devices available that support that conclusion. If Psalm 8 may be understood as *not* referencing collective humanity, then the passage would not be considered to assert a present tense dominion of humanity over nature.

A PROPOSAL: THE ADVANTAGE OF REDACTED DOMINIONISM

Recall the four basic interpretations of the dominion mandate: (1) dominionism, which appeals to the dominion mandate of Genesis 1:26–28 as a continuous prescription that places humanity over nature as its governor; (2) redefined dominionism, or the stewardship interpretation, which appeals to the conditions of Genesis 2, in which humanity exercises less mastery and more care over nature, as one would care for a garden—this interpretation normally softens the meaning of the rule and subdue terminology; (3) the citizenship interpretation, which focuses on human origin from the dirt and thus represents mankind as an equal member of the biotic community, and which recognizes anthropocentrism as the original sin which brought creation to corruption; and (4) redacted dominionism, an interpretation in which dominionism was the inaugural condition of humanity in its perfect state, yet because of the Fall that dominion was removed in light of human disqualification and consequent lack of ability to carry out the mandate. Whereas dominionism, stewardship, and citizenship each

6. Werther postulates, "I do not think that a positive difference in kind is a necessary and/or sufficient condition for functional superiority . . . The hierarchy of existent entities begins with inorganic substances, and rational substances to God. Both humans and angels are rational finite substances. But angels differ in kind from humans such that angels are ontologically superior to humans. However, angels are functionally inferior to humans. Angels serve humans. If ontological superiority were a sufficient condition for functional superiority then humans would serve angels." Werther, "Reason and the Imago Dei," 327.

have significant contextual flaws, redacted dominionism seems to avoid the inconsistencies the other three do not.

Dominionism handles well the rule and subdue imperatives of 1:26–28, but fails to integrate the changed conditions of post-Fall reality with the grounding for the commands. In particular, if the dominion mandate is based on qualification and ability stemming directly from the *imago Dei*, then if it is an enduring prescription one would expect some explanation of how Adam's image can be added to the ontological gene pool, so to speak, without directly affecting the qualification and ability of mankind to rule (5:3), and how the subsequent judgments of qualification and ability do not alter the *imago Dei* sufficiently to invalidate the mandate (6:5, 13). Additionally, this view must account for why the dominion mandate is later excluded and seemingly replaced simply by a proliferation mandate (9:7). Thus dominionism as the inaugural and temporary condition is not to be rejected. Enduring dominionism, on the other hand, seems within EC framework to be textually untenable.

Stewardship accommodates the pastoral implications of Adam's creation from the dirt (2:7), and of his role in the garden as cultivator and keeper (2:8, 15), but it is deficient in two particular ways. First, the stewardship interpretation is not consistent with the rule and subdue language of Genesis 1:26–28, which verbiage in its basic lexical sense references governance and sovereignty—even domination. Second, like dominionism, stewardship does not account for post-Fall teleology, because it is based on the pre-Fall conditions of Genesis 2. Just as post-Fall dominionism is not textually justified in Genesis, neither is post-Fall stewardship.

Part of the curse resulting from sin was a much less responsive earth (3:17–19) than the one in which the animals came willingly to Adam and fruits were plentiful for the taking (2:19–20). Further, special accommodations for man's survival in a post-Fall world were necessary (Gen 8–9). Of course, certain stewardship ideas do hold true to the text: humanity is to be responsible and to use resources wisely because God provides them; thus the concept of stewardship is not to be dismissed in its entirety. Only insofar as it is considered the enduring primary ontological grounding of human relation to nonhuman nature is stewardship problematic.

Citizenship handles especially well the scourge of anthropocentrism and its role in the Fall, but its dismissal of the Genesis 1 account and its failure to acknowledge the metaphysical distinction between human and nonhuman creates what would seem an insurmountable tension for the EC as defined in the introduction to this project. The *imago Dei* is too significant a quality uniquely imbued in humanity to consider all of nature metaphysically indistinct. While citizenship does not attempt to coordinate the first two chapters of Genesis, citizenship is the only view of the three (including dominionism and stewardship) that gives appropriate attention to the monumental and universal changes that accompanied the Fall. Additionally, the citizenship idea commendably attempts to diagnose the problem, and it does so without compromising the Fall narrative.

These three attempts at ascertaining the Genesis portrayal of human relation to nonhuman nature, if nothing else, at least underscore several factors desirable in an exegetically compatible (with the EC) and environmentally sympathetic understanding of Genesis. First, the interpretation should be consistent with the rule and subdue language of Genesis 1:26–28. Second, the interpretation should not dismiss the metaphysical distinction between human and nonhuman creation. Mankind was described uniquely made in the image of God, the consequences of which condition are diminished to the hurt of textual integrity.

Third, the interpretation should account for the drastic post-Fall alteration in the human and nonhuman condition. Failing to acknowledge this central shift in the course of events neglects the source of physical and spiritual death as well as the only biblical explanation for the present condition of humanity in relation to its environs. The significance of this causality is considered by the Apostle Paul, who asserts in Romans 5:12 that "through one man sin entered the world." The term translated *sin* (ἁμαρτία, hamartia), appears in its various forms some two hundred and thirty three times in the NT and the Hebrew equivalent (הטאת, *ḥaṭa't*) appears no less than two hundred and ninety-five times in the HB. It is a central theme—both textually and theologically—and it profoundly affects not only mankind's relation to God, but also human relation to nature. Fourth, the interpretation should account for the absence and seeming replacement of the dominion mandate in favor of the more limited in scope reproduction and proliferation mandate.

Of the four interpretive conclusions, redacted dominionism uniquely accommodates these four factors. It acquiesces to the most literal, despotic interpretation of Genesis 1:26–28, recognizing that the verbiage describes conditions in which humanity is indeed intended to govern the rest of nature. It acknowledges the ontological distinction between human and nonhuman nature by virtue of humanity's relation to the *imago*

Dei, recognizing that while there is some relation between the two (e.g., Adam's relation to the dirt in Genesis 2:7), humanity is essentially one thing and nature is another. It emphasizes the Fall as a pivot point that altered substantially the human relation both to God and to nature, and recognizes that even spiritual regeneration does not in the short term reverse all of the consequences of the Fall (in EC understanding, this kind of comprehensive reversal is a still yet future part of God's redemptive plan for the heavens and the earth and its contents). Finally, it recognizes and accounts for the fundamental distinctions between the original mandate for unfallen humanity and the revision for fallen humanity.

Redacted dominionism refers simply to an understanding of the early biblical narrative regarding the human relation to nature as follows: God created man and woman in a perfect state and commissioned them to govern nature as God's qualified and able representatives. They failed to fulfill the commission, and ironically their failure was expressed in an act that involved the misuse of a natural resource. The consequences about which God had forewarned them came about, and humanity's qualification and ability to govern (among other things) changed completely, leaving creation an utter mess with no qualified or able member remaining who might direct and manage nature appropriately. The entire creation remains in this forlorn condition until its creator resolves the issue—a resolution understood by the EC to be explained and anticipated in other portions of the Bible. Man's present responsibility is to continue fruitful existence, *without hindering the fulfillment of that same responsibility shared by the remainder of nature*, and to look to the creator for guidance and provision in resolving both the spiritual and temporal consequences insofar as they may be resolved.

As redacted dominionism is consistent with the textual evidence of Genesis and anticipates an exegetically derived grounding for a biblical environmental ethic, it is also consistent with a theocentric rather than anthropocentric understanding of the Genesis account. This is significant, because White's (for example) primary accusation against the creation story is that it is inherently anthropocentric, in its attribution of intrinsic value to humanity and instrumental value to the remainder of nature.

Some interpreters have understood Genesis to impute intrinsic value to all created things by way of the stewardship interpretation of the dominion mandate. Callicott views this as at least somewhat advantageous,[7] and considers that Genesis may indeed be understood to promote intrinsic value of nonhuman things,[8] though he acknowledges both views are textually plausible.[9] He comments further, "There is, however, a countercurrent of thought powerfully and discernibly running in the text of Genesis itself, however little representation it may have enjoyed in subsequent theology and popular Christianity . . . Within the general outlines of the traditional scriptural worldview, nonhuman species may have intrinsic value because they are parts of God's creation and God has conferred intrinsic value upon them, either by creating them or by a secondary fiat."[10] As Callicott recognizes here, the stewardship approach attempts to level the playing field between human and nonhuman nature, imbuing both with a degree (albeit an unequal one) of intrinsic value.

Redacted dominionism uniquely offers a theocentric understanding that implies that no part of creation needs to possess intrinsic value, but rather the entirety of creation possesses *instrumental value*, serving God's purposes, and his alone. Redacted dominionism, then, is a plausible means of answering also White's claim that nature is intended to serve only man's purposes. Regarding human valuation, Callicott observes that, "The God of the Judeo-Christian tradition is transcendent, not immanent. The hypothesis of such a God therefore permits us to conceive of intrinsic value as determined objectively, that is, from some point of reference outside of human consciousness."[11] Here Callicott recognizes that God can be understood to be the entity making definitive value assignments. Building on his idea, a further adjustment of human and nonhuman value from intrinsic to instrumental is only a slight maneuver here, and helps to resolve tensions inherent in the most commonly held interpretations of the dominion mandate.

Further, redacted dominionism avoids the anthropocentric themes requisite with the dominionist and stewardship models by recognition of a theocentric cosmology—a system in which God values things (human and nonhuman) as he pleases and for his own purposes and with no consideration for the things themselves, but only for how he uses them for

7. Callicott, "Non-Anthropocentric Value Theory," 302.

8. For example Callicott, *Defense of the Land Ethic*, 137.

9. Ibid., 138.

10. Ibid., 137.

11. Ibid.

his own doxological purpose. Thus, in the redacted dominionism model, things have value because they are God's things, and because he values them. The key environmental ethical consequence of redacted dominionism, then, is found in the idea that all created things are accountable to their creator for how they interact with other created things, irrespective of any intrinsic value ranking system, because all created things possess the same instrumental value (albeit with different functions) to the one who created them. As such, redacted dominionism offers a textually viable nonanthropocentric grounding for a biblical environmental ethic within an EC framework. Consequently, for those outside of the EC, redacted dominionism may prove to be a valuable catalyst for dialogue and a means whereby those outside the EC may hold the EC accountable for their own methodologies and environmental impact.

Bibliography

Abravanel, Rabbi Isaac. *Principles of Faith: Rosh Amanah*. Translated by Menachem Kellner. Oxford, UK: Littman Library of Jewish Civilization, 2000.

Altmann, Alexander. "Homo imago Dei." *Journal of Religion* 48, no. 3 (July 1968) 235–59.

Aristotle. *Politics: A Treatise on Government*. Translated by William Ellis. London: George Routledge and Sons, 1895.

Armstrong, Karen. *A History of God: The 4000-Year Quest of Judaism, Christianity, and Islam*. New York, NY: Random House, 1993.

Arndt, William, and F. Wilbur Gingrich. *A Greek-English Lexicon of the New Testament and Other Early Christian Literature: A translation and adaptation of Walter Bauer's Griechisch-Deutsches Worterbuch zu den Schriften des Neuen Testaments und der ubrigen urchristlichen Literatur, Fourth Revised and Augmented Edition 1952*. Chicago, IL: University of Chicago Press, 1957.

Attfield, Robin. "Christian Attitudes to Nature." *Journal of the History of Ideas* 44, no. 3 (July–September 1983) 369–86.

Augustine. *City of God*. Book 7, Chapter 11. No Pages. Online: http://www.newadvent.org/fathers/120108.htm.

———. *On Christian Doctrine*. Grand Rapids, MI: Christian Classics Ethereal Library.

Bacon, Francis. *The New Atlantis*. Edited by Charles W. Eliot. New York: P. F. Collier & Son, 1909.

———. *New Atlantis and Great Instauration*. Edited by Jerry Weinberger. Illinois: Harlan Davidson, 1989.

The Barna Group. No Pages. Online: www.barna.org/about.

———. "Evangelicals Go 'Green' with Caution." September 22, 2008. No Pages. Online: http://www.barna.org/barna-update/article/13-culture/23-evangelicals-go-qgreenq-with-caution.

Barth, Karl. *Church Dogmatics*. Vol 3:1. Edinburgh: T & T Clark, 1958.

Barton, John. *Understanding Old Testament Ethics*. Louisville, KY: Westminster John Knox Press, 2003.

Ben Isaiah, Abraham, and Benjamin Sharfman. *The Pentateuch and Rashi's Commentary: A Linear Translation into English*. Brooklyn, NY: S. S. & R. Publishing, 1949.

Bentham, Jeremy. *An Introduction to the Principles of Morals and Legislation*. No Pages. Online: http://www.econlib.org/library/Bentham/bnthPML1.html.

Berkhof, Louis. *Systematic Theology*. Grand Rapids, MI: Eerdmans, 1974.

Berry, Wendell. "Christianity and the Survival of Creation." In *Seeing God Everywhere*, edited by Barry McDonald, 53–72. Bloomington, IN: World Wisdom, 2004.

Biblia Hebraica Stuttgartensia: With Westminster Hebrew Morphology. Electronic ed. Stuttgart; Glenside PA: German Bible Society; Westminster Seminary, 1996, c1925; morphology c1991.

Bird, Phyllis A. "'Male and Female He created Them': Gen 1:27b in the Context of the Priestly Account of Creation." *Harvard Theological Review* 74, no. 2 (April 1981) 129–59.

Blaising, Craig, and Darrell Bock. *Progressive Dispensationalism*. Grand Rapids, MI: Baker Books, 1993.

Blinde, Per. "Nature in Roman Catholic Tradition." *Anthropological Quarterly* 74, no. 1 (January 2001) 15–27.

Bouma-Prediger, Steven. *For the Beauty of the Earth: A Christian Vision for Creation Care*. Grand Rapids, MI: Baker Books, 2010.

Brettler, Marc. "Rendsburg's 'The Redaction of Genesis.'" *Jewish Quarterly Review*, New Series 78, no. 1/2 (July–October 1987) 113–19.

Briggs, C. A. "The Hebrew Poem of the Creation." *The Old Testament Student* 3, no. 8 (April 1884) 273–88.

Brown, Francis, et al. *Enhanced Brown-Driver-Briggs Hebrew and English Lexicon, electronic ed.* Oak Harbor, WA: Logos Research Systems, 2000.

Bruce, F. F. *The Canon of Scripture*. Downers Grove, IL: IVP Academic, 1988.

Bullmore, Michael A. "The Four Most Important Biblical Passages for a Christian Environmentalism." *Trinity Journal* 19 NS (1998) 139–62.

Callicott, J. Baird. *Beyond the Land Ethic: More Essays in Environmental Philosophy*. New York, NY: SUNY Press, 1999.

———. *In Defense of the Land Ethic*. Albany, NY: SUNY Press, 1989.

———. *Earth's Insights: A Multicultural Survey of Ecological Ethics from the Mediterranean Basin to the Australian Outback*. Berkeley, CA: University of California Press, 1994.

———. "Genesis Revisited: Murian Musings on the Lynn White, Jr. Debate." *Environmental History Review* 14, no. 1/2, 1989 Conference Papers, Part 2 (Spring–Summer 1990) 65–90.

———. "Non-Anthropocentric Value Theory and Environmental Ethics." *American Philosophical Quarterly* 21, no. 4 (October 1984) 299–309.

Calvin, John. *Institutes of the Christian Religion*. Vol. 1. Philadelphia, PA: Westminster Press, 1960.

Charles, R. H. "A New Translation of the Book of Jubilees. Part 1." *Jewish Quarterly Review* 6, no. 1 (October 1893) 184–217.

Chazan, Robert. "The Barcelona 'Disputation' of 1263: Christian Missionizing and Jewish Response." *Speculum* 52, no. 4 (October 1977) 824–42.

Cohen, Abraham. *The Psalms: Hebrew Text & English Translation with an Introduction and Commentary*. London: Soncino Press, 1965.

Cohen, Jeremy. "The Bible, Man, and Nature in the History of Western Thought: A Call for Reassessment." *Journal of Religion* 65, no. 2 (April 1985) 155–72.

Collins, John C. "The Wayyiqtol as 'Pluperfect': When and Why." *Tyndale Bulletin* 46.1 (1995) 117–40.

Colwell, Ernest Cadman. "Biblical Criticism: Lower and Higher." *Journal of Biblical Literature* 67, no. 1 (March 1948) 1–12.

Couch, Mal, ed. *Classical Evangelical Hermeneutics*. Grand Rapids, MI: Kregel, 2000.

De Beer, E. S., ed. *The Correspondence of John Locke*. Vol. 2. Oxford: Clarendon Press, 1979.

Descartes, Rene. *Discourse on Method and Meditations on First Philosophy*. Translated by Elizabeth S. Haldane. Mineola, NY: Dover Publications, 2003.

DeWitt, C. B. "Behemoth and Batrachians in the Eye of God: Responsibility to Other Kinds in Biblical Perspective." In *Christianity & Ecology: Seeking the Well-Being of Earth & Humans*, edited by Dieter T. Hessel and Rosemary Radford Ruether, 291–316, manuscript copy. Cambridge: Harvard University Press, 2000.

Eckburg, Douglas Lee, and T. Jean Blocker. "Varieties of Religious Involvement and Environmental Concerns: Testing the Lynn White Thesis." *Journal for the Scientific Study of Religion* 28, no. 4 (December 1989) 509–17.

Enderle, Georges. "In Search of a Common Ethical Ground: Corporate Environmental Responsibility from the Perspective of Christian Environmental Stewardship." *Journal of Business Ethics* 16, no. 2 (1997) 173–81.

English Standard Version Bible. Wheaton, IL: Crossway Books, 2001.

Enns, Paul. *The Moody Handbook of Theology*. Chicago, IL: Moody Press, 1989.

Erickson, Millard. "Biblical Theology of Ecology." In *The Earth is the Lord's*, edited by Richard Land and Louis Moore, 36–54. Nashville, TN: Broadman Press, 1992.

Evangelical Theological Society. No pages. Online: http://www.etsjets.org/about.

Faramelli, Norm. "Whither the Bible in Environmental Ethics and Moral Argument." *Journal for the Study of Religion, Nature, and Culture* 3, no. 2 (June 2009) 266–70.

Feenstra, Ernest S., et al. "Christian Impact on Ecology." *Science*, New Series 156, no. 3776 (May 12, 1967) 737–38.

Feldman, Louis H. "Josephus' Portrait of Moses." *Jewish Quarterly Review*, New Series 82, no. 3/4 (January–April 1992) 285–328.

Fortin, Ernest L. "The Bible Made Me Do It: Christianity, Science, and the Environment." *Review of Politics* 57, no. 2 (Spring 1995) 197–223.

Fox, Stephen. *The American Conservation Movement: John Muir and His Legacy*. Madison, WI: University of Wisconsin Press, 1986.

Friere, Paulo. *Pedagogy of the Oppressed*. Translated by Myra Bergman Ramos. New York, NY: Continuum, 2006.

Gaebelein, A. C. *The Annotated Bible, Vol. I: The Pentateuch*. New York, NY: Our Hope, 1913.

Gaebelein, Frank, ed. *The Expositor's Bible Commentary, Volume 5: Psalms—Song of Songs*. Grand Rapids, MI: Zondervan, 1991.

Geisler, Norman L. *Inerrancy*. Grand Rapids, MI: Zondervan, 1980.

Geisler, Norman L., and William E. Nix. *A General Introduction to the Bible*. Chicago, IL: Moody Press, 1986.

Gerstner, John. *Wrongly Dividing the Word of Truth*. Morgan, PA: Soli Deo Gloria, 2000.

Goodpaster, Kenneth. "On Being Morally Considerable." *Journal of Philosophy* 75 (1978) 308–25.

Graves, Robert, and Raphael Patai. *Hebrew Myths: The Book of Genesis*. New York, NY: Greenwich House, 1983.

Guth, James L., et al. "Faith and the Environment: Religious Beliefs and Attitudes on Environmental Policy." *Journal of Political Science* 39, no. 2 (May 1995) 364–82.

Guthrie, W. K. C. *A History of Greek Philosophy, Volume II: The Presocratic Tradition from Parmenides to Democritus*. London: Cambridge University Press, 1965.

Hand, Carl M., and Kent D. Van Liere. "Religion, Mastery-Over-Nature, and Environmental Concern." *Social Forces* 63, no. 2 (December 1984) 555–70.

Hanson, Victor Davis. *The Other Greeks: The Family Farm and the Agrarian Roots of Western Civilization.* New York, NY: Free Press, 1995.

Hargrove, Eugene. "Weak Anthropocentric Intrinsic Value." In *Environmental Ethics*, edited by Andrew Light and Holmes Rolston III, 175–90. Malden, MA: Blackwell, 2003.

Harris, R. L., et al. *Theological Wordbook of the Old Testament.* Vol. 1. Chicago, IL: Moody Press, 1980.

Harrison, Peter. "Subduing the Earth: Genesis 1, Early Modern Science, and the Exploitation of Nature." *Journal of Religion* 79, no. 1 (January 1999) 86–109.

Hayes, Bernadette C., and Manussos Marangudakis. "Religion and Environmental Issues within Anglo-American Democracies." *Review of Religious Research* 42, no. 2 (December 2000) 159–74.

Hiebert, Theodore. "The Human Vocation." In *Christianity and Ecology.* Cambridge, MA: Harvard University Press, 2003.

Hiers, Richard H. "Reverence for Life and Environmental Ethics in Biblical Law and Covenant." *Journal of Law and Religion* 13, no. 1 (1996–1999) 127–88.

Hobbes, Thomas. *Leviathan.* Edited by Richard Tuck. Cambridge, UK: Cambridge University Press, 1996.

Hughes, James A. "Another Look at the Hebrew Tenses." *Journal of Near East Studies* 29, no. 1 (January 1970) 12–24.

Hull, R. Bruce. *Infinite Nature.* Chicago, IL: University of Chicago Press, 2006.

Hume, David. *Enquiries Concerning Human Understanding and Concerning the Principles of Morals.* New York, NY: Oxford University Press, 1975.

Irenaeus. *The Demonstration of the Apostolic Preaching.* New York, NY: MacMillan, 1920.

Jamieson, R., et al. *A Commentary on the Old and New Testaments.* Vol 1. Peabody, MA: Hendrickson, 2002.

Jastrow, Morris, Jr. "The Hebrew and Babylonian Accounts of Creation." *Jewish Quarterly Review* 13, no. 4 (July 1901) 620–54.

Jonas, Hans. *The Phenomenon of Life: Toward a Philosophical Biology.* New York, NY: Dell Publishing, 1966.

Josephus, Flavius. *The Works of Josephus Complete and Unabridged.* Translated by William Whiston. Peabody, MA: Hendrickson, 1987.

Kanagy, Conrad L., and Hart M. Nelson. "Religion and Environmental Concern: Challenging the Dominant Assumptions." *Review of Religious Research* 37, no. 1 (September 1995) 33–45.

Kant, Immanuel. *Lectures on Ethics.* Edited by Peter Heath and J. B. Schneewind. Cambridge, UK: Cambridge University Press, 1997.

Kay, Jeanne. "Human Dominion over Nature in the Hebrew Bible." *Annals of the Association of American Geographers* 79, no. 2 (June 1989) 214–32.

Kearns, Laurel. "Saving the Creation: Christian Environmentalism in the United States." *Sociology of Religion* 57, no. 1, *Special Issue: Sociology of Culture and Sociology of Religion* (Spring 1996) 55–70.

Keil, C. F., and F. Delitzsch. *Commentary on the Old Testament, Volume 1: The Pentateuch.* Peabody, MA: Hendrickson, 2001.

———. *Commentary on the Old Testament, Volume 5: Psalms*. Peabody, MA: Hendrickson, 2001.

Keller, David R., ed. *Environmental Ethics: The Big Questions*. Malden, MA: Blackwell, 2010.

Kelley, Page. *Biblical Hebrew: An Introductory Grammar*. Grand Rapids, MI: Eerdmans, 1920.

Kennington, Richard. *On Modern Origins: Essays in Early Modern Philosophy*. Lanham, MD: Lexington Books, 2004.

Kittel, Bonnie Pedrotti, et al. *Biblical Hebrew: A Text and Workbook*. New Haven, CT: Yale University Press, 1989.

Kosmin, Barry A., and Ariela Keysar. *American Religious Identification Survey Summary Report, March 2009*. Hartford, CT: Trinity College, Institute for the Study of Secularism in Society and Culture, 2009.

Kuyper, Abraham. *Keep Thy Solemn Feasts: Meditations by Abraham Kuyper*. Grand Rapids, MI: Eerdmans, 1903.

Lampert, Laurence. *Nietzsche and Modern Times: A Study of Bacon, Descartes and Nietzsche*. New Haven: Yale University Press, 1993.

Land, Richard, and Louis Moore. *The Earth is the Lord's*. Nashville, TN: Broadman Press, 1992.

Leopold, Aldo. *A Sand County Almanac and Sketches Here and There*. New York: Oxford University Press, 1989.

Leupold, Herbert C. *Exposition of Genesis*. 2 vols. Grand Rapids, MI: Baker Books, 1984.

Lewis, Gordon R., and Lewis Demarest. *Integrative Theology*. Vol. 3. Grand Rapids, MI: Zondervan, 1996.

Lightner, Robert. *Handbook of Evangelical Theology*. Grand Rapids, MI: Kregel, 1995.

Lin, Timothy. *Genesis: A Biblical Theology*. 4th ed. Carmel, IN: Biblical Studies Ministries International, 2002.

Lust, Johan, et al. *A Greek-English Lexicon of the Septuagint: Revised Edition*. Electronic edition. Stuttgart: Deutsche Bibelgesellschaft, 2003.

Maimonides, Moses. *Commentary on the Mishnah, Tractate Sanhedrin*. Translated by Fred Rosner. New York, NY: Sepher-Hermon Press, 1981.

Marshall, John. *John Locke: Resistance, Religion and Responsibility*. Cambridge, MA: Cambridge University Press, 1994.

Mazar, Benjamin. "The Historical Background of the Book of Genesis." *Journal of Near Eastern Studies* 28, no. 2 (April 1969) 73–83.

McDonald, Barry. *Seeing God Everywhere*. New York, NY: World Wisdom, 2004.

McGinn, Bernard. "Asceticism and Mysticism in Late Antiquity and the Early Middle Ages." In *Asceticism*, edited by Vincent L. Wimbush and Richard Valantasis, 58–74. New York, NY: Oxford University Press, 1998.

McHarg, Ian L. "The Place of Nature in the City of Man." *Annals of the American Academy of Political and Social Science*, vol. 352, Urban Revival: Goals and Standards (March 1964) 1–12.

McKnight, Stephen. *The Religious Foundation of Francis Bacon's Thought*. Columbia, MO: University of Missouri Press, 2005.

Mead, Frank, and Samuel Hill. *Handbook of Denominations*. 9th ed. Nashville, TN: Abingdon Press, 1990.

Merrill, Eugene. "Genesis 1–11 as Literal History." In *The Genesis Factor*, edited by Ron. J. Bigalke Jr., 75–92. Green Forest, AR: Master Books, 2008.

Mill, John Stuart, and Jeremy Bentham. *Utilitarianism and Other Essays*. Edited by Alan Ryan. New York, NY: Penguin, 1987.

Minear, Paul S. "How Objective is Biblical Criticism?" *Journal of Bible and Religion* 9, no. 4 (November 1941) 217–22.

Morris, Henry M. *The Genesis Record: A Scientific and Devotional Commentary on the Book of Beginnings*. Grand Rapids, MI: Baker Books, 1976.

Nash, James A. "The Bible vs. Biodiversity: The Case Against Moral Argument from Scripture." *Journal for the Study of Religion, Nature, and Culture* 3, no. 2 (June 2009) 213–37.

Nash, Roderick Frazier. *The Rights of Nature*. Madison, WI: University of Wisconsin Press, 1989.

Nietzsche, Freidrich Wilhelm. *The Gay Science*. Edited by Bernard Williams, translated by Josefine Nickhauff. Cambridge, UK: Cambridge University Press, 2001.

Noll, Mark. *A History of Christianity in the United States and Canada*. Grand Rapids, MI: Eerdmans, 1992.

Northcott, Matthew. "Loving Scripture and Nature." *Journal for the Study of Religion, Nature, and Culture* 3, no. 2 (June 2009) 247–53.

Norton, Bryan. "Environmental Ethics and Weak Anthropocentrism." In *Environmental Ethics: An Anthology*, edited by Andrew Light, 163–74. Malden, MA: Blackwell, 2003.

O'Neill, John. "Varieties of Intrinsic Value." In *Environmental Ethics*, edited by Andrew Light and Holmes Rolston III, 131–42. Malden, MA: Blackwell, 2003.

Paterson, Timothy. "On the Role of Christianity in the Political Philosophy of Francis Bacon." *Polity* 19, no. 3 (Spring 1987) 419–42.

———. "The Secular Control of Scientific Power in the Political Philosophy of Francis Bacon." *Polity* 21, no. 3 (Spring 1989) 457–80.

Pegis, Anton. *Introduction to Saint Thomas Aquinas*. New York, NY: Random House, 1948.

Philo. *The Works of Philo: New Updated Edition*. Edited and translated by C. D. Yonge. Peabody, MA: Hendrickson, 1993.

Plato. *Lysis, Symposium, Gorgias*. Translated by W. R. M. Lamb. Cambridge, MA: Harvard University Press, 2001.

———. *The Republic of Plato*. Translated by Benjamin Jowett. Vol 1. London: Oxford University Press, 1927.

———. *Timaeus and Critias*. Translated by Robin Watterfield. New York, NY: Oxford University Press, 2008.

Poole, Matthew. *A Commentary on the Holy Bible, Volume I: Genesis–Job*. Peabody, MA: Hendrickson, 1985.

Rahlfs, Alfred. *Septuaginta*. Stuttgart: Deutsche Bibbelgellschaft Stuttgart, 1979.

Ramm, Bernard. *Protestant Biblical Interpretation*. Grand Rapids, MI: Baker Books, 1970.

Rand, Ayn. *The Virtue of Selfishness*. New York, NY: Penguin, 1964.

Rand, Benjamin, ed. *The Correspondence of John Locke and Edward Clarke*. Cambridge, MA: Harvard University Press, 1927.

Randolph, Richard, and Jeremy Yunt. "Cal DeWitt and the Evangelical Approach to Environmental Ethics." No pages. Online: http://www.counterbalance.net/enviro/calvi-frame.html.

Rendsburg, Gary A. *The Redaction of Genesis*. Winona Lake, IN: Eisenbraun, 1986.

Rich, John, and Andrew Wallace-Hadrill, eds. *City and Country in the Ancient World*. New York, NY: Routledge, 1991.

Rivkin, Ellis. "The Internal City: Judaism and Urbanization." *Journal for the Scientific Study of Religion* 5, no. 2 (Spring 1966) 225–40.

Roberts, Alexander, and James Donaldson, eds. *Ante-Nicene Christian Library: The Writings of Tertullian*. 11 vols. Edinburgh: T & T Clark, 1867–1873.

Roberts, David. "An Interview with Environmental Scientist and Evangelical Leader Calvin DeWitt." No pages. Online: http://grist.org/article/dewitt/.

Rogerson, John William. *Genesis 1–11*. New York, NY: T & T Clark, 2004.

Rolston, Holmes, III. *Considering Natural Value*. New York, NY: Columbia University Press, 1994.

Rosenberg, Shalom. "Concepts of Torah and Nature in Jewish Thought." In *Judaism and Ecology*, 189–219. Cambridge, MA: Harvard University Press, 2002.

Ross, Allen. "Genesis." In *The Bible Knowledge Commentary: Old Testament*, edited by John F. Walvoord and Roy B. Zuck, 15–103. Colorado Springs, CO: Victor, 2004.

Ryrie, Charles C. *Dispensationalism Today*. Chicago, IL: Moody Press, 1965.

———, ed. *The Ryrie Study Bible: New American Standard Translation*. Chicago, IL: Moody Press, 1978.

Sacks, Robert. *The Lion and the Ass: A Commentary on the Book of Genesis*. Lewiston, NY: Edwin Mellen, 1990.

Sagan, Carl. *Billions and Billions: Thoughts on Life and Death at the Brink of the Millennium*. New York, NY: Ballantine, 1997.

———. *Cosmos*. New York, NY: Ballantine, 1980.

———. "The Shores of the Cosmic Ocean." Episode 1 in *Cosmos: The Complete Collection*. Turner Home Entertainment, 1996.

Samuelson, Norbert M. "Rethinking Ethics in the Light of Jewish Thought and the Life Sciences." *Journal of Religious Ethics* 29, no. 2 (Summer 2001) 209–33.

Saucy, Robert. *The Case for Progressive Dispensationalism*. Grand Rapids, MI: Zondervan, 1993.

Schaff, Philip, ed. *The Nicene and Post-Nicene Fathers of the Christian Church, Vol. II: St. Augustin's City of God and Christian Doctrine*. Grand Rapids, MI: Eerdmans, 1988.

Schwandt, John, and C. John Collins, eds. *The English-Greek Reverse Interlinear New Testament: English Standard Version*. Wheaton, IL: Crossway Books, 2006.

Septuaginta: With Morphology. Stuttgart: Deutsche Bibelgesellschaft, 1996, c1979.

Shereshevsky, Ezra. "The Significance of Rashi's Commentary on the Pentateuch: Book 1." *Jewish Quarterly Review*, New Series 54, no. 1 (July 1963) 58–79.

Smith, Suzanne. "The New Atlantis: Francis Bacon's Theological-Political Utopia?" *Harvard Theological Review* 101:1 (2008) 97–125.

Strong, Augustus. *Systematic Theology*. Philadelphia, PA: Judson Press, 1947.

Tan, Paul Lee. *The Interpretation of Prophecy*. Dallas, TX: Bible Communications, 1974.

Taylor, Paul W. "The Ethics of Respect for Nature." In *Environmental Ethics: The Big Questions*, edited by David R. Keller, 175–81. Malden, MA: Blackwell, 2010.

Taylor, W. R. "Biblical Criticism and Modern Faith." *Journal of Religion* 23, no. 4 (October 1943) 229–39.

Terry, Milton. *Biblical Hermeneutics: A Treatise on the Interpretation of the Old and New Testaments*. Grand Rapids, MI: Zondervan, 1976.

Tertullian. *De Anima*. No pages. http://www.newadvent.org/fathers/0310.htm

———. *De Resurrectione Carnis*. No pages. Online: http://www.newadvent.org/fathers/0316.htm

———. *De Spectaculis*. No Pages. Online: http://www.newadvent.org/fathers/0303.htm

Tuck, Richard. "The Utopianism of *Leviathan*." In *Leviathan After 350 Years*, edited by Tom Sorrel and Luc Foisneau, 125–39. Oxford: Oxford University Press, 2004.

Vilkka, Leena. *The Intrinsic Value of Nature*. Atlanta, GA: Rodopi B. V., 1997.

Wallis, Louis. "The Paradox of Modern Biblical Criticism." *Biblical World* 52, no. 1 (July 1918) 41–49.

Waltke, Bruce. *Genesis: A Commentary*. Grand Rapids, MI: Zondervan, 2001.

Warfield, B. B. *Evolution, Scripture, and Science: Selected Writings*. Edited by Mark A. Noll and David N. Livingstone. Grand Rapids, MI: Baker Books, 2000.

Weinberger, J. "Bacon's Utopia: An Introduction to the Reading of the New Atlantis." *American Political Science Review* 70, no. 3 (September 1976) 865–85.

Wenham, John. "Christ's View of Scripture." In *Inerrancy*, edited by Norman Geisler, 3–38. Grand Rapids, MI: Zondervan, 1980.

Werther, David. "Animal Reason and the Imago Dei." *Religious Studies* 24, no. 3 (September 1988) 325–35.

White, Lynn Townsend, Jr. "Christian Myth and Christian History." *Journal of the History of Ideas* 3, no. 2 (April 1942) 145–58.

———. "Continuing the Conversation." In *Western Man and Environmental Ethics*, edited by Ian Barbour, 55–65. Reading, MA: Addison-Wesley Publishing, 1973.

———. "The Historical Roots of Our Ecologic Crisis." *Science* 155, no. 3767 (March 1967) 1203–7.

———. "Natural Science and Naturalistic Art in the Middle Ages." *American Historical Review* 52, no. 3 (April 1947) 421–35.

Williams, Michael Allen. *Rethinking Gnosticism: An Argument for Dismantling a Dubious Category*. Princeton, NJ: Princeton University Press, 1999.

Woodrum, Eric, and Thomas Hoban. "Theology and Religiosity Effects on Environmentalism." *Review of Religion Research* 35, no. 3 (March 1994) 193–206.

Wright, Richard T. "Responsibility for the Ecological Crisis." *BioScience* 20, no. 15 (August 1, 1970) 851–53.

Yaffe, Martin. *Spinoza's Theologico-Political Treatise*. Newbury Port, MA: Focus Philosophical Library, 2004.

———, ed. *Judaism and Environmental Ethics: A Reader*. Lanham, MD: Lexington Books, 2001.